A NEW BEGINNING

David Swarbrick

TotalRecall Publications, Inc.
1103 Middlecreek
Friendswood, Texas 77546
281-992-3131 281-482-5390 Fax
www.totalrecallpress.com

All rights reserved. Except as permitted under the United States Copyright Act of 1976, No part of this publication may be reproduced, stored in a retrieval system, or transmitted in any form or by any means electronic or mechanical or by photocopying, recording, or otherwise without prior permission of the publisher. Exclusive worldwide content publication / distribution by TotalRecall Publications, Inc.

Copyright © 2015 by David Swarbrick
All rights reserved

ISBN: 978-1-59095-464-5
UPC: 6-43977-44645-9

Printed in the United States of America with simultaneous printing in Australia, Canada, and United Kingdom.

FIRST EDITION
1 2 3 4 5 6 7 8 9 10

The scanning, uploading and distribution of this book via the Internet or via any other means without the permission of the publisher is illegal and punishable by law. Please purchase only authorized electronic editions, and do not participate in or encourage electronic piracy of copyrighted materials. Your support of the author's rights is appreciated.

This book is dedicated to anyone, regardless of: race, creed, social status, or political views. Who, has ever pondered as to why with all of humanities great knowledge and awesome technological advancements, that "we," as a "species," can build marvelous looking buildings. We can manipulate and control atoms, genetics, and alter our environment to suit our needs. We can launch people into space. We can land on the moon and send probes to study far-off worlds. We can also map distant star systems, and catalog hundreds upon hundreds of other planets outside of our very own star system. But yet, in spite of just some of these great achievements, throughout generations after countless generations, a large majority of us still waste our lives fighting over "Imaginary" Gods and "Delusional" ideas. We build weapons to kill and supposedly protect ourselves from evildoers and trespassers, and yet, in the "Free," world of humanity, when one of our own falls sick and lands on "Ill's" door. We run, we hide, we blame, we pray, we debate, we gossip, and yet we still can't figure out the easiest, most logical way to pay for and take care of them.

David…

About The Book

Mark Morgan is a famous writer. He has everything his heart could desire: money, a nice house, a nice vacation home, cars, and a beautiful loving wife who'd recently become pregnant. It was all anyone could ever dream of or hope for, and he was the happiest person that one could ever be. All things were going good for him; his books were selling faster than they could be shelved, he won a couple of awards, and he and his wife were going to have the little girl that he had always wanted. For the both of them it was true bliss. One day after tragedy strikes for the second time, Mark loses himself and almost everything else. His wife and unborn child are killed, his uncle, who was his best friend for so long is gone. He doesn't care about his career or himself anymore, hopelessness sets in, he soon becomes mentally ill, and he just can't find the will or strength to move on. Kara, his wife was the only person in his life besides his mother and uncle that he had ever truly loved, and now that they're both gone, will he ever be the same, and will he be able to live his life and truly love anything or anyone else ever again?

Join Author David Swarbrick in this dramatic twisting tale of love, loss, and one man's struggle to start a new beginning…

Foreword

A New Beginning by David Swarbrick was a wonderfully written story about love, loss and new beginnings. Mark's losses and battles are emotionally riveting and touching. They will make you laugh, cry and ask why did that happen. This book is a page turner. Once you start you will not be able to stop.

C. Jarvis

Aspiring author, Accounting Major, and Process technician.

Introduction

Standing over his uncle's casket as it slowly lowered into the ground, Mark Morgan's mind raced back through memory after memory of the strong relationship the two of them had shared. With every bright flashback that snapped on and off through his conscious imagination, Mark also kept reliving the confusing tragedy that had led him to this point in his life. *Why did this have to happen?* He thought, *and is this nightmare ever going to end? I sure hope so.*

He also tried his hardest not to cry, but he just couldn't hold it in….

Mark was your typical thirty-two year old man. He was around 5'8" tall, and weighed 175 pounds. He was slim and well built, had short dark brown hair, and the deepest, dark brown eyes one could ever gaze into. He was basically an all-around good-looking and quite charming guy, which really drove the ladies wild. Of course there was only one lady for him, and that lady was his beautiful wife Kara; to whom he had been happily married for eight years, and who had just recently became pregnant.

Kara being the lovely woman she was, stood around 5'6" tall, was medium framed, and was very curvy. She had long, straight beautiful auburn colored hair, that was thick with healthiness, and always had a glistening shine to it. She also had the brightest emerald-green eyes that stood out against her soft, pale skin and sparkled like two shiny priceless jewels. Most people, male or female, could at times become mesmerized just by looking into them, and one could say that in a way, she had sort of an elegant vampirish look to her. Add that into her warm motherly smile, and she could heat the coldest of cold days in most anyone's heart. No matter how cold or alone one felt, when Kara smiled her smile, and spoke in her soft sensuous voice, she could usually pull anyone from the deepest darkest places that life or circumstances had taken them.

This usually worked for Mark as well, but today, the day he had thought he had finally put his uncle and the past two years of tormenting heartache to rest, was a day Kara's warm smile, deep green eyes, and ever-so-soft caress, just wouldn't work. Nor did she try to make it work either, because she, too felt herself to be in a very cold and alone place. And even though for the past two years they'd had a lot of love and strong support from family and friends, the both of them, mainly Mark, still felt alone and cold. It was almost as if time had stopped, and something from a faraway place was slowly taking small pieces of their existence, and little-by-little, piece-by-piece replacing it with a poison that slowly ate away and rotted their warm fiery souls into a pot of lifeless sickness. The kind of sickness that makes a person just not want to live anymore, that's the way Mark was feeling, more so than Kara. With every racing thought, with every old and new memory, Mark, with Kara by his side, just blankly stared while a Holy man spoke, and the casket finally rested at the bottom of a cold, concrete vault.

Mark wondered if this was finally the end…

No, one part of his mind said, *it will never be over.*

Yes, another part of his mind said, *it's finally done.*

I don't believe you, another part of his mind said.

Why did this have to happen? Why do I have to be here? It wasn't supposed to end like this…. Why did this happen??? It all could have been prevented. Mark's mind kept repeating and racing, will things ever slow down and work out right??? I don't know man, I feel so sick…

1

Standing over his uncle's casket as it slowly lowered into the ground, Mark Morgan's mind raced back through memory after memory of the strong relationship the two of them had shared. With every bright flashback that snapped on and off through his conscious imagination, Mark also kept reliving the confusing tragedy that had led him to this point in his life. *Why did this have to happen?* He thought, *and is this nightmare ever going to end? I sure hope so.*

He also tried his hardest not to cry, but he just couldn't hold it in....

Mark was your typical thirty-two year old man. He was around 5'8" tall, and weighed 175 pounds. He was slim and well built, had short dark brown hair, and the deepest, dark brown eyes one could ever gaze into. He was basically an all-around good-looking and quite charming guy, which really drove the ladies wild. Of course there was only one lady for him, and that lady was his beautiful wife Kara; to whom he had been happily married for eight years, and who had just recently became pregnant.

Kara being the lovely woman she was, stood around 5'6" tall, was medium framed, and was very curvy. She had long, straight beautiful auburn colored hair, that was thick with healthiness, and always had a glistening shine to it. She also had the brightest emerald-green eyes that stood out against her soft, pale skin and sparkled like two shiny priceless jewels.

Most people, male or female, could at times become mesmerized just by looking into them, and one could say that in a way, she had sort of an elegant vampirish look to her. Add that into her warm motherly smile, and she could heat the coldest of cold days in most anyone's heart. No matter how cold or alone one felt, when Kara smiled her smile, and spoke in her soft sensuous voice, she could usually pull anyone from the deepest darkest places that life or circumstances had taken them.

This usually worked for Mark as well, but today, the day he had thought he had finally put his uncle and the past two years of tormenting heartache to rest, was a day Kara's warm smile, deep green eyes, and ever-so-soft caress, just wouldn't work. Nor did she try to make it work either, because she, too felt herself to be in a very cold and alone place. And even though for the past two years they'd had a lot of love and strong support from family and friends, the both of them, mainly Mark, still felt alone and cold. It was almost as if time had stopped, and something from a faraway place was slowly taking small pieces of their existence, and little-by-little, piece-by-piece replacing it with a poison that slowly ate away and rotted their warm fiery souls into a pot of lifeless sickness. The kind of sickness that makes a person just not want to live anymore, that's the way Mark was feeling, more so then Kara. With every racing thought, with every old and new memory, Mark, with Kara by his side, just blankly stared while a Holy man spoke, and the casket finally rested at the bottom of a cold, concrete vault.

Mark wondered if this was finally the end…

No, one part of his mind said, *it will never be over.*

Yes, another part of his mind said, *it's finally done.*

I don't believe you, another part of his mind said.

Why did this have to happen? Why do I have to be here? It wasn't supposed to end like this…. Why did this happen??? It all could have been prevented. Mark's mind kept repeating and racing, will things ever slow down and work out right??? I don't know man, I feel so sick… I still have to finish paying for this fucking funeral!! I sure hope there's some money left… Oh thank goodness, it's finally over…

2

One month before the death of his uncle, Mark fell under enormous amounts of stress, and this stress started to affect his health, his home life, and his relationships with his friends, family, and wife. He even started having horrible panic attacks that led to days and days of nervousness, paranoia, and sometimes even uncontrollable vomiting. He was sick, and he was also completely slacking off on his work. Work that he had for a long time, held very dear to himself, and also took very seriously. But during the whole ordeal with his uncle, the state, the uncle's estate, the uncle's finances, the uncle's bills, the uncle's health care, lawyers, state workers, collection agencies, doctors, and nursing homes, he just couldn't get it together and take it, nor really much of anything else too seriously.

You see Mark was a writer, and he still is, and he's also a very good one at that. It wasn't something that happened over night for him, though. For years, probably ever since he was a little boy, Mark struggled to find his place. He never did well in school, he never really had many friends, he never really had much interest in what the majority of his peers were interested in; which made it difficult for him to fit in, but fitting in was also something Mark never really cared about. He still doesn't. He was always somewhat of an outsider.

He went to college and managed to get an Associate's Degree in Photography and Applied Science, but he never really did anything with it. He wasn't passionate enough about it. He only picked that course of study because he thought he could and would make a good paycheck from it; which he probably could have if he'd had the passion that he needed in order to become successful. But he didn't, so shortly after college, he found himself bouncing for a few years from job to job. Some good, some bad, and some, downright lousy. Things really stunk for Mark, and he knew they stunk. But what could he do? He had no clue, so he just kept going with what he could get. It wasn't until shortly after he met Kara, that he had finally found his calling, and fully knew what he was supposed to do, and going to do with the rest of his life.

One night while at work, Mark looked around the convenience store he had been employed at, and in his mind he heard this marvelous children's story play out. He heard it play out so plainly, that it was like someone was directly reading it to his mind. So when he got home later that evening, he grabbed a tablet and wrote the whole story down. He then spent a few days editing and revising the story, which he did quite a few times. Soon after that, he found a publisher that was willing to turn the story into a book. Then within a year, Mark had his first book released to the public. Shortly after that, he wrote two more children's books, and three adult novels, which were also released to the public. Over time all of them did fairly well, and it seemed to Mark as though he had found his place. And he did. And he felt really good about it, it, and life itself was all good. But for some reason when tragedy struck, Mark became very depressed, and had his doubts. Not just doubts about his writings or his books; he had doubts about everything. Everything, including life itself; he was very confused.

3

It was a Mid-November afternoon in Mid-Michigan, the sun was out, the air was crisp and cool. The sky was a deep blue, and a few white clouds hung silently in the pre-wintery background. Mark and Kara had been out late the prior evening, so they were just getting up and about and starting their day.

Walking around their modest home, while Kara began to prepare them both something to eat, Mark started to open some curtains in the main living room of their house. But before he finished, Mark was interrupted by a knock on the front door. So he stopped what he was doing, made his way to the door and looked through the peephole. Surprised to see that it was his uncle's landlord, Mark quickly opened the door and found himself being told the sad news. News that would have a heart-wrenching effect on not only his own life, but the lives of Kara, his uncle, and many others for quite some time. So heart-wrenching, and downright confusing, that Mark, within a year's time and at Kara's requests, found himself-searching for and seeking professional help from a qualified therapist. After some research, he and Kara found a female doctor that the both of them agreed on, and also thought could do Mark some good. She was a local therapist. Named Doctor Susan Downs, she sounded to Mark and Kara to be very promising. She was thirty-nine years old, and had a Master's Degree in Counseling, Psychology. She was licensed through the state in which they lived as a Limited Licensed Psychologist. She had fifteen years of experience. She worked with ages seven through adult in an outpatient setting. She was an M.A. An L.L.P. a C.A.A.C...

Her areas of special interest were, adolescents/Christian counseling/grief /loss issues/ victims of abuse/eating disorders/ chronic pain/ depression/ anxiety/ obsessive compulsive disorders/stress management/crisis resolution.

She had also published a few different papers on new treatments for people with varied levels of mental illnesses, that were caused from various life-changing trauma. These papers had won her several different awards from many different medical institutions.

At first, Mark had been hesitant about seeing the doctor. He and Kara had even debated over whether or not he would go through with it. After he finally agreed, he found himself thinking, *Man, I hope this is worth it...*

4

Session one

Sitting in a large waiting room on a very uncomfortable wood chair that was covered with green padding, Mark stretched his legs out and casually looked around the room. He mentally examined various items such as end tables, magazine racks, hanging plants, precisely hung pictures, plaques, and Exit and Enter signs. While he looked, Mark tried not to look the other people in the room in the eye, nor at the office assistants that were shuffling around as they did their work. Not that he was embarrassed to be there; he just didn't want anyone to think he had some sort of a staring problem. He was very uncomfortable and his mind raced and bounced from thought to thought. He had no clue as to what he should expect.

Sliding his feet across the rough green carpet beneath his shoes, Mark slid his legs back, and thought as he crossed his ankles over one another, *Wow, there's a lot of people here... Craziness must be going around these days. Man I hope no one recognizes me. I feel so stupid... Do I really need to be here? Yes you promised Kara. Yeah I did, didn't I?*

Taking a quick glance at a clock on the wall adjacent to him, Mark thought again, Man, for only being here ten minutes, it sure as hell seems like it's been a lot longer.

"Mark Morgan." A stern, but rather feminine female voice then called from behind him.

"Yeah, that's me." Mark replied as he stood up, turned around, and immediately saw a strawberry blond-haired woman with glasses leaning through an open door that she held open with her left elbow.

She was wearing a very nice-looking light blue business dress, and, "Right this way," she said with a smile.

Making his way to the open door while the woman turned around, Mark stepped through and followed her down a long hallway.

Quickly coming to an open door, Mark casually followed the woman through and looked around at what was obviously her office.

The woman said, "Please, have a seat and make yourself comfortable."

Stepping to a very nice looking couch, Mark sat down and looked around some more. He quickly gazed at the various items that were perfectly placed and neatly nestled around the office.

The woman stepped to a desk and sat down on a very comfortable looking black padded chair with small wheels.

She pushed a lever and adjusted the chair's back, and said as she looked at Mark with a smile, "Okay, now that's done. My name is Susan, and you're obviously Mark, right?"

"Yep, that's me."

"Okay then. I've read the assessment paperwork you filled out before your scheduled appointment, and from what I've gathered, you're having some problems with severe anxiety and depression."

"Oh yeah, I sure am."

"Any thoughts of suicide?"

"No," Mark replied with a smile, "never, but if a few people I knew did commit suicide, I can't say I would be sad about it."

"Well, sometimes, when one's angry, it's normal to think that way. Unless the thoughts are overwhelming, then feeling that way could become a danger. Are they overwhelming?"

"No, they're not overwhelming, the thoughts, just like the racing thoughts I keep experiencing lately, come and go."

Doctor Susan adjusted her glasses and said, "Well, experiencing anger is human. However, overbearing anxiety and depression is a problem, and I'm here to help you with that, and to also teach you some coping methods. That way we can hopefully avoid psychiatric meds, because I'm a firm believer that if they can be avoided, then by all means, avoid them. What do you think?"

"Oh yeah I agree, and I would like to definitely avoid any, if not all the meds I can."

"Okay good…. Now what do you think triggered your symptoms, the emotions, the anxiety and depression, or when it all started?"

"Oh, I know when it all started. That was a while ago. I'd been feeling lousy for quite some time. But it really didn't affect me too much. It wasn't until about a month ago that those feelings started to have a big effect on me and the people around me."

"Okay then, lets go back to where you would say it all started." Doctor Susan then leaned back and crossed her legs together while Mark carried on.

"Well about a year and a half ago I got a knock on the door. It was my uncle's landlord. He lived… He meaning my uncle, lived in a mobile home park that's only a few blocks from my house. I hadn't heard from him in a long time. At least two years. He acted like he wanted nothing to do with me or anyone else. So after a short time of trying to stay in contact and keeping up to date with him, I gave up, which really hurt for a long time. Because for the longest time we were the best of friends. I had thought for a long time that I did something wrong, but there was another side of my mind that was telling me I didn't do anything wrong, and that there was something wrong with him. I just couldn't prove it. So like I said before, I gave up on him."

"How did that make you feel?"

"Terrible," Mark replied, "and helpless. My guts told me he was sick and needed help, and I wanted so badly to help him. But there was nothing I could do, he refused help. I even called Adult Protective Services to help him, but when they went to his home, he threw them out."

"What made you think he needed help, and why did you call A.P.S.?"

"Because he had a different look in his eyes. Now I'm not a professional, but I knew what I saw... And what I saw wasn't good......"

"Well, go on. What did you see?"

Mark leaned to the side of the couch, slid his feet around, and said, "What I saw was the look of complete madness, and I don't mean anger. He had, and still does have, and I know that this is a cruel way to put it, but he's got the look of a loony person. You know; the look of someone that's slowly losing their mind, or has already lost it. That's what he looked like, and I don't care who you are, you know that look when you see it.... Something was terribly wrong with his mind, so I called

A.P.S... Plus he was living in complete, downright, and totally disgusting filth. But yet like I said before, he threw them out, and they told me if he's not a threat to himself, then there's nothing they can do. Yeah right, I'd say when a man has lost his mind, and he's living in a home that's caked in human urine, blood, garbage, and feces, that he's a threat to himself, and his neighbors. Wouldn't you?"

"Yes I would say so."

"Thanks for agreeing with me," Mark replied and said as he sat back up. He kept moving around like he was really uncomfortable, "People are so fucking stupid....Anyways... When I spoke with his landlord, he told me that he hadn't heard from John..."

"John being your uncle?" Doctor Susan asked.

"Yes, that's correct. He hadn't seen or heard from him in about ten days, and the last time he'd seen John, he looked really, really bad."

"Bad as in being sick?"

"Yep, that's right.. As a matter of fact, the landlord said that."

Mark's mind as he leaned forward momentarily flashed back to the conversation he had with John's landlord, and for a moment it was like he was there all over again having the same exchange.

"The last I'd seen him, John looked like death warmed over," The landlord had said.

"I'll go down and see what's going on….." Mark cleared his throat, and flashed back into where he really was, leaned back, and continued. "I really didn't want to go though."

"Why?"

"Because I had, had a bad feeling, and so did Kara."

"Kara?"

"My wife."

"Okay, sorry."

"I also kind of knew what was going to happen, and also what I was gonna find. You just sometimes know these kind of things…. You know what I mean?"

"Oh yeah, I sure do." Doctor Susan replied. She also cleared her throat, reached to her desk, and took a sip from a cup of water while Mark carried on.

"Anyways, rather than go down there, I decided to call his house. But after about fifty rings and numerous tries, no one answered. Of course I didn't expect anyone to either. So after about an hour of dragging my feet, Kara convinced me to go and check things out. A lot of good that was gonna do though. I didn't have a key, that's what the landlord originally wanted, he wanted to know if I had a key so he could let himself in to see if John was okay. But I didn't have one. I used to though. When I gave up on John I threw it out. Bad mistake. Maybe, who knows? Anyways, so I got myself together, I was somewhat nervous, I drove down to the trailer park and made my way to John's trailer. Then after about ten minutes of banging on the doors and trying to see into a couple of windows, I gave up and pulled out the old cell phone, dialed 911, and told them the situation. Soon after, the local township pigs arrived and I told them the situation. They too knocked on doors, asked neighbors questions, made phone calls and looked through windows. The whole time I was thinking,*("What? You people think I was fucking lying or something?")* I had already did what they were doing, and I told them that.. Idiots, they refused to immediately kick the door in. They needed proof that John was in the home, and that he was hurt, which was and is understandable. I could have kicked it in myself but I didn't, and the reason I didn't was because if I did and I found John dead, the cops probably would have found a way to make me their number one suspect."

"Why do you say that?"

Mark leaned forward and replied, "Because that's what they do."

Doctor Susan looked at Mark with sort of a puzzled look; she was curious as to what was going through his head. He was obviously angry. She said, "That's sometimes true…" She paused. "I get the feeling you don't really care for law enforcement people."

"No not really. To me they're just another example of how sick our society really is." Mark leaned back again, his tone changed, and Doctor Susan asked.

"Why do you say that?"

"Well in my opinion, a true clean, and intelligent society that had people living in it with any kind of common sense, wouldn't need them in the first place, and there would be no such thing. But that's just my opinion, and I don't want to debate it."

"Okay, maybe we'll debate that another time?"

"Maybe."

"So what happened next?"

"Well after they screwed around for a little while longer, one of the officers, who I think was, and still is a fucking jerk-off, managed to spot John through a crack in the curtains of a small bathroom window. He was lying on the floor almost dead. So they finally kicked the door in and soon after called an ambulance. When they went in, he was lying in his own waste, he was hypothermic, and he had two humongous bed sores that were completely infected. He was totally incoherent, and he only weighed about one hundred pounds."

"Wow! Sounds pretty traumatic. How old was he when this took place?" Doctor Susan asked as Mark shuffled his feet and said.

"He had just turned sixty two, but he looked much older. When I went to see him at the hospital the next day, I didn't even recognize him."

"How did that make you feel?"

"Well even though at the time I was extremely pissed off, it really frightened me. So much that it made me sick to my stomach…. To see someone you've known, loved, and respected for most of your life in the shape he was in, can be, and was, a very gut-wrenching experience. He looked just like a helpless child, and what I consciously and unconsciously found to be the most frightening about the whole thing was, he also looked like complete madness. Even his home felt like madness, after I went in the night before to close and lock it up, it just dripped off from everything. Everything that was directly or indirectly in contact with him."

"By madness, do you mean anger?"

"No. Like I said before, madness like insanity, or some sort of mental illness. It must have just kicked in and taken over his mind or something. And by the look he had in his eyes, I know it did. Like I also said before, I just couldn't prove it."

"Was he ever given a psychiatric exam?"

Mark sat up and said, "Yeah, the hospital eventually did

one. But it wasn't determined until quite sometime later that along with the large tumor he had in his colon, and the problem he had developed with his throat, that he was in the second stage of dementia, which had probably started a few years prior and slowly progressed with time."

Doctor Susan uncrossed her legs and sat up as well; she said, "Yep, that's how dementia starts. With some, its been known to start as early as their mid-thirties. It's even been known to regress with treatment, if caught in time. But in most cases, cases probably such as your uncle's, it can take years to progress, and the more recognizable symptoms will usually go unnoticed until a later age. Then it usually ends up being too late. It sounds like you spotted them though."

"Yeah, if only he would have accepted the help when I tried to get him help, none of this, more than likely would have happened."

"Maybe, it's hard to say. Try not to blame yourself for any of it though. Remember, he was sick."

"Yeah I know," Mark somberly replied, "and I try not to. In fact I try every day, and I know something could have been done to prevent it, and I know its not my fault, but I…"

"And it wasn't your fault. Some things, especially when it comes to mental illness, illness such as your uncle John's can't be helped."

"Yeah I know, I just wish I could fully convince myself of that. One part of me says it wasn't my fault. Another part says it was, and it drives me nuts."

"Well the part of you that says it was needs to go away. In fact, that's why we're here. We're here, and we're gonna make that side quiet down. Here's a tip: Whenever you start to hear what I call, "the opposing negative side of your mind," try to picture the positive side as a large creature that can quickly snatch the negative side up and tape its mouth shut."

"Ha ha, ha," Mark laughed and said, "that sounds pretty eerie, and also funny at the same time."

"In a way, but if you practice it enough, you'll find that it should work." Doctor Susan replied with a voice of encouragement; she could tell by Mark's body language that he was, and had been really frustrated. It also made her feel good to have made him laugh.

"Okay," Mark said with enthusiasm, "and thanks. I'll give it a try."

"Good, now tell me. Hmm?" Doctor Susan thought for a moment... "You said that the next day you had went to the hospital to visit your uncle, and that you were, well in your words, "extremely pissed off." Did that, your anger have anything to do with what had happened, or was it over something else?"

"Hmm?...." Mark thought for a moment... And said, "No, it was over what had happened. Well sort of...." Mark sat thinking again.

"Mark?"

"I'm thinking about how to put it."

"You know you can speak freely, and anything you say is all confidential."

"Yeah I know. I just..... Man! Every time I think about it I get mad again."

"Don't bottle it up, let it out, and I guarantee you'll feel better."

"Yeah I know." Mark leaned back and took a deep breath.

Doctor Susan said, "Well come on, spill it, Dude."

"Dude?"

Doctor Susan laughed and said, " Yeah Dude, now out with it."

Mark also laughed and said, "Well, since you put it that way. The day everything took place with John, one of the officers that was there. Fucking dickhead! The jerk that had eventually kicked the door in, and was also the first one to get to my uncle, spent the first ten minutes of his arrival time checking out John's car, which included checking the tag and running the fucking plate. Why he did this I have no clue, it was fucking stupid."

"Why did that make you so mad?" Doctor Susan asked as she sat back and crossed her legs again. .

Mark replied, "Because John's life, and I'm not saying this because it was my uncle's life that was hanging in the balance; I'd say it regardless of who it was, and this idiot that calls himself a civil servant, and wears a stupid badge of honor, acted more worried about a goddamn car then another human's life. What a bunch of shit! You're there to possibly save a life, and your first concern is their car, give me a fucking break!"

Doctor Susan could sense Mark's anger again, his tone was filled with excitement, and what he had said really didn't make much sense to her; she asked, "So you were mad because that person acted more concerned with the car than your uncle's wellbeing?"

"Yes!"

"That would be frustrating. Did you make a complaint?"

"No."

"Why? I mean, if you felt that strongly about it, you could

have made one, and should have."

"Because I knew it wouldn't have done any good."

"It might have made you feel better."

"Yeah, but I doubt it."

"Why's that?"

"Because there's more to the story," Mark replied, "plus I was so mad that if I had made a complaint, I probably would have been arrested. Man, I wanted to punch that fucker in the nose so bad! Especially after what took place the next day. Like I said, there's more to the story." Mark was starting to turn red.

Doctor Susan said, "Carry on."

"Well the next day before I went to see John, I got a phone call from the local township's code enforcement officer, and he said that he had been informed that there was a junk car sitting at my uncle's residence and it had to be removed. And if it wasn't, he would have to issue a violation citation. Plus, if repairs weren't made to the trailer, he would have to tag it as uninhabitable. Which, I understood the trailer part; that place was screwed up. But the car, that made absolutely no fucking sense. The car wasn't junk. Yeah it was a little beat up, but it had legal plates, tags, and insurance, and it was drivable. And according to their stupid township ordinance, that's all a vehicle needs in order to sit out for a lengthy period of time."

"Did you tell the code enforcement that?"

"Yeah I did, but for some stupid reason he started bitching about the doughnut tire that was on the back passenger side. So I just said, "Whatever," and hung up on the prick. I wasn't going to keep arguing with a moron. Especially one that wasn't making any sense. So I went and got the car, I legally drove it home, and I parked it in my garage until I decided to get rid of it. That way there would be no more whah, whah, about it sitting there."

"Well I can certainly see why you were mad."

"Yeah, really?" Mark asked as he sat back up, "Well thank you. I still can't believe it though, a man almost died, and all these people wanted to do was whine about a car.. Small-minded fucks.. I also still wonder why that stupid cop made such a big deal over that car, and let alone had to fucking lie about it. You know, I understand that people make mistakes. Hell, I make them all the time, and most people have a job to do. But when things get tough and a tragedy happens, don't do things to make one's life harder. Especially, like I said before, a man almost died and ended up in critical condition, and all you want to do is make a gripe over a hunk of worthless steel. What a joke! Cars can be replaced; people can't. Humans sometimes are so fucking stupid…"

Mark showed anger and aggression with what he had said, so much, as to which, in order to calm him, Doctor Susan immediately replied as she uncrossed her legs and sat up straight. "Yes, you're so right, sometimes they are, and that's why when you find yourself in a confusing situation, and you find yourself becoming so angry and confused that you can't stand it, that it's usually best to steer that anger and confusion towards a quick and simple solution, which you did."

"What do you mean?"

"Well," Doctor Susan replied while she spoke with her hands, "rather then punch the opposing person in the nose and let the argument with the code enforcement officer escalate into something worse, you obviously thought of a simple solution to the problem, and quickly removed it."

"I don't get it?"

Mark was puzzled…

Doctor Susan replied, "Well it's human nature to take petty things such as the issue with your uncle's car, and make them escalate into huge dilemmas, which often leads to controversy. But by cutting the man off and just moving the car without saying anything else about it, you stopped what could have, and more than likely would have, escalated into something much bigger than what it needed to be. And honestly, that's probably what they wanted, and also expected. And I know at the time, you probably thought that they started this whole thing, and that you shouldn't have to even be dealing with it."

"Exactly!" Mark said with excitement.

He no longer felt puzzled…

Doctor Susan carried on, "Yeah, but you did, and you obviously finished it before they knew what had been done. So you, not them, made the right choice. Um, did you ever speak to them again?"

"Nope, they called, but I never returned their call. I guess though, the landlord was asked about the car, and he did ask me about it, and I said, "Why, what car? It's gone, why keep bringing it up?"

"Good. Now are you still mad about it?"

"No, not really," Mark was calmer, "I still sometimes try to figure out why the cop was so concerned with the car, but the more I talk about it, the more it seems to fade."

"That's a good thing," Doctor Susan replied, "and with time it should bother you less and less. Just remember, don't dwell on yesterday, live for today and strive for tomorrow."

"I'll try and keep that in mind."

"Good then," Doctor Susan cheerfully replied as she looked at her wristwatch, "times up, and I'll see you in five days. If you don't mind, you can leave the door open on your way out."

"Nope, not at all." Mark replied.

"Alright, I'll see you."

"Bye."

Mark got up and left the room while Doctor Susan grabbed a pen and pad of paper from her desk, wrote some things down, thought for a moment, then went and called on her next case.

5

Session 2

Five days later

Stepping into her office and closing the door behind her, Doctor Susan made her way to her chair and smiled at Mark; who was sitting in the room patiently waiting for her.

She sat down and asked as she faced him with a warm smile, "So how are we; well I take it?"

"Yeah I'm alright." Mark replied somberly.

"Okay, good. Anything new happen since the last time we spoke?"

"No not really, everything's pretty much still the same."

"Okay, well let me see…." Doctor Susan paused and thought for a few seconds. Her stomach had been bothering her all day, and it was sort of making it hard for her to concentrate on things. "Okay, the last time we spoke I asked you to tell me about when you think your symptoms started. Which you did, and mind you, you did it very well. But that's when you said you think they started. But they actually didn't trigger and kick in until about a month ago. So, lay it on me; what happened to trigger everything?"

"Well…. Hmm? Okay let me think…." Mark paused for a moment, sat back, and said, "Alright, I told you about how things with my uncle started, and how it affected me then… But things, especially for him, got worse. And I say seventy-five percent of it was brought on by people and the stupid rules they make and follow….."

"Okay, well carry on." Doctor Susan leaned back in her chair, and Mark carried on.

"Well John obviously ended up in the hospital. In fact he was in intensive care for at least a month. I think… Hmm, it might have been longer, everything's somewhat a bit fuzzy. Anyways, man they had him hooked to all sorts of things. He was even on a feeding tube, and I don't mean the kind that goes through the nose and down the throat. This one was hooked right into his small intestine. It was horrible-looking. I hated seeing him like that. Part of me, if I could have, would have traded places with him. But we all know that would have been impossible."

"Yeah that's true. Go on."

"Anyways, he was there for quite a while, and he looked like shit. No one thought he was gonna make it. A few times before they put the feeding tube in him he almost didn't."

"How so?" Doctor Susan asked while she thought, *God, my stomach is killing me!*

"Well the hospital tried to let him eat on his own. Not once but twice, and each time he aspirated and almost choked to death. That's obviously why he ended up on the feeding tube."

"Did the hospital ever determine the cause?"

"The cause?" Mark asked as he leaned forward.

"The reason he kept choking?"

"Oh yeah, sorry." Mark felt stupid. "They claimed there was something wrong with his Epiglottis, and it was inoperable.

Which I think was a lie, I just couldn't prove it."

"Why do you think that?"

"Well even though he ended up not needing surgery on it, because now he's eating just fine, I think they lied because he didn't have any health insurance, and they wouldn't operate on him without it. I also think that's why they didn't do the surgery he needed to have to remove the tumor from his colon that doctors found while he was there. And the reason that I say all of that is because after the huge bed sores he had healed, and he no longer needed to be in intensive care, the hospital shoved him off to a rehab/nursing home. Which mind you, was thirty miles away and in a different county."

"Wow! Really, why?" Doctor Susan asked with a surprised tone.

Mark replied, "Because none of the local places would take him without health insurance. Which I think is, or was, one of the, and notice I said, "One," one of the most fucked-up, absurd things I had ever heard. He had money, he could have paid straight out-of-pocket to be at one of the places that refused him. But nope; he had to have insurance, and because of them stupid people, not because of me, I had to drive sixty miles every time I had to take care of his business. It was crazy. I still find myself asking, "Why?" I mean, it's downright crazy that our society bases one's care and wellbeing on what insurance he or she holds. Or whether they have it or not."

"You're right, and I totally agree with you. Health care is something our society needs to desperately work on."

"You're telling me." Mark said with a sarcastic tone, "You wouldn't believe what we had to go through just to get it for him."

"We being...?"

"My wife and I."

"Oh okay. I'm sorry."

"That's okay."

"If you don't mind me asking?"

"No go ahead."

"Why didn't your uncle have insurance? I mean, even though you're right, and I totally agree with you that it shouldn't have mattered. Why didn't he have it?"

"Well," Mark said, "he had just recently retired early. He had, and still has Charcot-Marie-Tooth disease, and due to that disease, which he was born with. It, the disease slowly progressed and got worse with age, so he had to stop working, he had no choice, and at the time he was, and still is receiving SSI benefits, and he hadn't been receiving the benefits long enough to get his Medicare part A and B..... For some stupid reason, and why this is, is way the fuck beyond me, you have to be receiving benefits for three months before you can get the insurance, and then sometimes you still may not qualify for it."

"Really! You're kidding me! I wonder why that is?"

"Who knows? I'll tell you though, it's really fucking nuts. There was a few times where I thought I was gonna lose my mind over the whole thing. It was crazy, and just think about this; you or anyone else, just like my uncle could find yourself really screwed if you got sick within those three months."

"Yeah, no kidding...Um?" Doctor Susan paused and thought for a moment. She then asked as she leaned forward, "Okay, lets change gears for a moment. Charcot-Marie-Tooth disease? I've never heard of it, so if you don't mind me asking?"

"No not at all." Mark replied.

"What is it?"

"Well, it's a rare form of Muscular Dystrophy that causes all kinds of problems in the lower extremities. Mainly the feet, calves, ankles, and sometimes the arms, hands and even the face muscles, which is hereditary, and like I said before, the disease progresses with age. But with exercise and a proper diet it is manageable, it's just not manageable with a bottle of booze. Drinking heavily is how he tried to manage it; obviously that didn't work…"

"Booze is really never a good way to manage anything…"

"Yeah, tell me about it…"

"Hmm, I'm curious? You said the disease is, "Hereditary," does anyone else in your family have it?"

"Oddly enough," Mark somberly replied, "no…"

Doctor Susan leaned back, crossed her legs; her stomach still hurt, and she said, "Yeah, that is odd? Hmm…Well, I'm going to have to do some studying because that's the first I've ever heard of that one. Thanks for educating me on it."

"You're welcome…" Mark somberly replied.

Doctor Susan then said, "Okay, back to your uncle's insurance problem. What about Medicaid, could he get that?"

"Nope, not during that time he couldn't. He has it now, but then they said he had too much money. Which he had, had some. But it wasn't nearly enough to pay all the hospital bills that started pouring in. Nope, no way. Just the time he spent in the first hospital built up to almost one hundred and fifty thousand dollars."

"The first hospital?" Doctor Susan asked with a surprised and confused tone.

Mark replied, "Yeah, shortly after he was practically

dumped at the first home that took him in, he ended up back in the hospital, but this was a different one. Not to disgust you or anything, but he was sent there for severe rectal bleeding, and almost bled to death. All because the first hospital didn't do the surgery he needed to remove the tumor he had in his colon. Plus the huge bed sores came back, because the nursing home wouldn't use the medicine vacuum that he needed for them. And it was all because he didn't have any insurance. So he spent another three weeks in another hospital, but this time the surgery was done, and the tumor was successfully removed. It was also there where it was determined that he was in the first stages of dementia."

"Well that was a good thing." Doctor Susan replied. She couldn't believe what she was hearing, and she sort of felt sorry for Mark.

Mark said, "Yeah it was, and is. I think? He was still in bad shape though, and still had no insurance. And he had to go back to the home that had taken him in, and he had refused to go back to that one."

"Why was that?"

"I have no clue. All he kept saying was…." Mark's mind flashed back to the moment he was talking about…. He was face to face with his sick uncle who was laying, and looking terrible, in a hospital bed. His uncle repeatedly said in a crazy, mumbling fashion, "They treat you wrong! They treat you wrong! You mother fucker! I wanna go back to the other place!"

There was no other place…..

Mark snapped out of the vision. He kept speaking, "There was no other place, and he would never elaborate on the, "They treat you wrong," comment. I tried to tell him he had to go back to that home because of his insurance situation. But he wouldn't listen.... He wouldn't listen to me... Nor would he listen to anyone else........." Mark then sighed and said, "Man, it was frustrating."

"I bet. So what happened?"

"Well, he was practically dumped into another home, another one that was another thirty miles away, and another county away. All because he refused to go back to the other one, and because he still didn't have any insurance, they were the only ones that would take him. So now in order to see him and take care of his business, my wife and I had to drive over sixty miles one-way. What an inconvenience that was, and I don't mean just for Kara and I, it was an inconvenience for him as well... Why is it that in our society, a man or a woman can work hard their whole lives, then end up having to go through what he, myself, and my wife had to, and are still going through? I mean really! " Mark was angry again, "You work hard for most of your life, if not all of your life, you pay into a system that's supposed be there for you when you're done, and when you are done, and if you get sick... But, if there's one little thing out of place, you're kicked around and shoved around like an old, worthless shoe. You know when someone, and I don't care who you are or what you've done, or what worth some loud-mouthed, self-centered fucking jerk-off has placed on you, you deserve the best. Don't you think?"

"Yes you do, and I can obviously see that, that makes you very angry."

"It's that obvious?"

"Yeah Mark, you're turning really red."

"Sorry." Mark replied.

He mindfully tried to calm himself down…

Doctor Susan said, "Don't be sorry, that's why we're here. You need to get those things off your chest…. Now I know you're a writer, I read it in your assessment file."

"Yep I sure am." Mark was calm again, he said, "Three children's books, and three adult novels, and, one of my novels just went to number one."

"Wow! Really? That's great! You and your wife must be really excited."

"No not really. I mean we are and were, Kara more than me, but you know with everything that's been going on, I have a really hard time even caring about much of it, or anything else. Is that normal?"

"Yes, it's normal," Doctor Susan said as she adjusted her glasses, "and very understandable. A lot of times when there's extra stress in our lives, stress that brings us down and wears us out, the things that really matter the most to us, mainly when the things that control our livelihood seem to spin out of control, can seem and feel unimportant. And when we feel like we're being brought down by outside forces that are out of our control, it can be very hard to get excited about things. But, if the down feeling won't go away, then there could be a deeper problem, and anti-depression meds might have to be prescribed."

"Oh boy, I sure don't want that. I've seen those meds screw a lot of people up and actually make them worse than they were before."

"Well don't worry Mark, we're going to try our best to avoid them."

"Good."

"Okay then…. Now the reason I brought up your writing is, sometimes writing can, for some people, be very therapeutic, and you, obviously already being in the book business, know how to get one published. So, why don't you write something that's based on our poor health care system? I mean, you've so far been through it, and you've obviously got some strong opinions about the system, so you should give it a try."

"You think?" Mark asked as he stretched out his feet.

"Oh yes, definitely…" Doctor Susan replied as she looked at her watch, and by that, Mark caught the hint that his session must be over.

Doctor Susan kept speaking "And I also think that if you do decide to try my idea, that you might find that by taking the negative in your life and turning it into something positive, it could and probably would make you feel better. And it could also give you back your sense of purpose, which I get the feeling that you've somewhat lost."

"Yeah, you are so right," Mark replied, "I have sort of lost my purpose. But you know what? Your idea sounds like a great idea, and I'm gonna give it a try. Thanks!"

"You bet. Good luck and I'll see you next week."

"Same place, same time?"

"Yes Mark; same place, same time."

"K, see you then, and thanks again."

"Again, you're welcome. You can shut the door this time if you don't mind?"

"Nope not at all. See you."

"Bye."

Mark got up and left the room while Doctor Susan uncrossed her legs, rolled her chair to her desk, folded open a lap top computer, and turned it on. She sat in deep thought for a moment, then stood up and looked through the blinds of her office window. She watched Mark get into his car and drive away. There was something different about him and his case; she couldn't put her finger on it. Something was different about it and him; different from all the other cases she'd ever had; Mark was different. There was something about him she just couldn't explain. Maybe it was her instincts or an over-active imagination, she just didn't know, but she felt like there was something more to him and he wasn't saying; it felt to her as if he was intently hiding something. What it was, she had no idea, and she had thought about it throughout their whole session, and now she couldn't stop thinking about it; what it was, was really boggling her mind.

After she stopped looking through the window shade, Doctor Susan shook off those thoughts, and thought, *Damn, why does my stomach hurt so bad. Maybe I should try to poop, that might help?* She then went to call in her next patient. She cut her session with this person short though, she couldn't concentrate on it; her thoughts kept dwelling on Mark's case, *What is it about him that's so different?* She kept thinking over and over again. It was almost driving her nuts; she couldn't stand it. So she made the excuse that she wasn't feeling well, and she would see the patient at a later date. She also canceled all of her other appointments for the day and went home early.

Driving home, she even blared her car stereo really loudly to try and drown out her thoughts. It didn't work; they just kept cycling about Mark over and over again. She didn't get it, *What the hell's going on? Why can't I stop thinking about him, and what is it that's so different?*

When she got home, again to try and quiet her mind, she went in and took a long nap.

Later that day in the early evening, Doctor Susan and her husband went to dinner at an upper-class restaurant. Over dinner Susan was a little quieter than normal; she was the type of person that liked to talk a lot, and her husband couldn't help but notice that she had seemed a little preoccupied with something, so he asked, "Susan, is there something wrong? You're not your normal talkative self."

"No, nothing's wrong."

"Are you sure?"

"Yeah... Well no. I mean nothing's wrong, I just have this case, and there's something about it that's just..."

"Just what?"

"It's just... I don't know, there's just something that's not adding up, and I don't know why. I mean there's nothing out of the ordinary; the case is pretty typical. There's just something different and I don't know what it is. I can sense it, and it's driving me nuts."

"Well I'm sure you'll figure it out."

"Maybe, I don't know. It's just weird, and it's probably just me."

"Well don't strain too hard, you're starting to crinkle your pretty face."

"That bad huh?"

"Yeah, you should see yourself. You're starting to freak me out."

"I'm sorry. You know what? I'll just forget about it so we can have a nice evening; it's probably nothing anyways."

"Okay, if that's what you want."

"Yes, most definitely."

"Good, then let's have a toast." Susan's husband raised his glass of wine and she raised hers as well, "To us, wealth, and good health."

"Here, here." Susan replied while they clicked their glasses together and took a sip, "I'll drink to that and many more." She took another sip, and she still kept thinking about Mark. Even after she said she would forget and have a good time, she didn't, she couldn't, her puzzling thoughts stuck with her the whole night, so she just faked her way through it the best she could. She didn't want to disappoint her husband and ruin everything for him, she loved him too much to do that; so she did her best to keep it to herself. It was his birthday, and she wanted him to enjoy it to his fullest, which he did. Susan's husband had a ball that night, and because she made sure of it, even though they both probably would have rather forgotten about it, it ended up being a night that he nor she wouldn't ever forget.

After dinner they went to a movie, and after the movie they went to a private local mixed strip club where they danced, partied, blew loads of money, drank gallons of booze, and smoked tons of dope until closing time. Things there got pretty rowdy, and they both got so intoxicated that they had to take a cab ride home. Susan wanted sex when they got in, so she immediately went to the kitchen, dropped her pants and her underwear, and bent over the kitchen table. But her husband was too wasted, when he dropped his pants and tried to give her what she had wanted, he couldn't. He couldn't get it up, and he just mumbled a drunken slur, looked at Susan's big bare butt with extremely blurred vision, and limply pressed himself against her. He grunted, "Whew," then fell over sideways with his pants down, hit the floor with a really loud thud, and immediately passed out. Extremely pissed off about it, Susan left him lay until the next morning. She stumbled off to use the bathroom, tried pulling her pants up on her way, and passed out as well. She passed out on the toilet while going pee, and eventually fell off it. She woke up the next morning on the floor with her pants and underwear still down around her ankles, and a splitting headache.

She, nor her husband went to work that day, nor did they talk much about the night before. They were both extremely hung over and somewhat embarrassed to even mention it. Susan that day also forgot about what it was that was so different about Mark's case; the excesses of the night before had somehow blocked it out.

Her mysterious stomachache was gone as well…

6

Session 3

Seven days after his second session with Doctor Susan, Mark went to his third session with somewhat of a different outlook on things. He felt a little more positive about life and his career, and the anxiety and worthlessness he had been feeling for so long had lightened up a little. It seemed as though the first two sessions had begun to help him, and the methods that Doctor Susan had suggested for him to use to lower his stress levels were somewhat working. So everything, he thought, including the wonderful relationship he'd had with his darling wife, would hopefully soon fall back into place and go back to normal. This was something Mark desperately wanted, but while he sat in Doctor Susan's office and patently waited for her to step in and sit down, Mark looked around the brightly lit room and his mind began to wonder.

Thinking about some of the events that had recently taken place with his uncle, Mark's heart began to pound, his hands started to shake, and he began to feel a deep painful pit in his stomach. Trying desperately to focus his mind on something other then the dilemmas of his uncle, Mark mentally struggled and tried to push the images and racing thoughts that were flashing through his mind's eye like a malfunctioning movie reel, to the side.

His attempts were futile…

No matter how hard he had tried to replace the negative thoughts with more positive ones, the negative ones just kept coming, and Mark soon found himself falling into a nasty daydream. One that Doctor Susan quickly startled him out of as she walked into the room, closed the door, and said before she sat down, "Mark. Mark.. Mark! Are you in there?"

"Huh! Yeah I'm in here."

"Well are you all right? You look like you were on another planet."

"I was, well sort of. I was just thinking...... Oh you know what, never mind."

"No never mind," Doctor Susan said, "if you were in a bad place or have something to say, then you need to get it out and say it."

"Yeah I know, I just...."

Mark paused and blanked out again...

Doctor Susan asked Mark with concern, because she really liked him for some reason. She found him to be really interesting, and she was genuinely concerned about him "You just what?"

Mark finally answered her, "Well even though the methods you told me to try when I find my anxiety levels rising are sort of working, I still find myself falling into daydreams and racing thoughts."

Doctor Susan leaned back in her chair and asked, "These daydreams and racing thoughts that obviously bring on the anxiety and panic attacks, do they always have something to do with your uncle?"

"Oh yeah, they sure do, and they're mostly about the more recent events; the ones that I think triggered all of this. We had started to talk about them, but we never finished."

"No we didn't," Doctor Susan said as she took her glasses off and cleaned the lenses with a piece of tissue, "but fortunately that's why we scheduled more sessions. So, lets start where you left off."

She finished cleaning them and put them back on...

Mark said, "Well, like I told you, John was put in another home, the tumor was successfully removed, he was still on a feeding tube because he couldn't swallow. He had the first stages of dementia, he couldn't walk or stand on his own anymore, and he still had no health insurance, and his bills were piling up. Remember?"

"Yeah, most of it. I don't remember you saying he couldn't walk or stand up on his own anymore though, but hey, that's okay, right?"

"Right." Mark replied.

"Okay then. I do remember though how angry his insurance situation and the whole health care system had made you. Have you tried writing about it like I had suggested?"

"Yeah I did, and as a matter of fact, that day when I got home I started writing about it. And thanks to you and your suggestion, I've decided to write a ninety-thousand word book on the whole subject."

"Well that's great! I'm happy for you! Now how does that make you feel?"

Doctor Susan leaned back in her chair and crossed her legs.

Mark said, "Hmm... You know I'm not really sure... Hmm, I guess I would have to say for now my emotions are mixed. Of course they're mixed on just about everything right now. But hopefully writing this new book will help straighten them out."

"Yes, good thinking. If you stick with the hopeful attitude you should find that the writing will work. But you have to want it to, because if you don't, then it probably won't work."

"Oh trust me, I want it to." Mark replied while he leaned back against the couch.

"Good, now tell me about the more recent events," Doctor Susan said with a smile.

Mark replied "Well, shortly after John was moved to another home, I, after going through some hoops, managed to get power of attorney over him, his medical decisions, his estate, and all of his finances. And don't ask me how I did it, but I even managed to get him the health insurance that he so much deserved."

"Good. Now how come you had to do all of that, didn't he have any other family? No brothers, sisters, or any children? You know, someone to help share the load?"

"Yeah he has brothers and sisters. His parents are both deceased, but no children, and I was the only one that wanted to do any of it. Of course they had no problem sticking their noses into everything; that's another story though. Anyways, I was always the closest to him, so I accepted and took on the responsibility of taking care of everything. Plus I knew damn well if I didn't, the state would have come along and taken everything he had. And if by some small miracle he had gotten better, he wouldn't have had anything to go home to. Let alone he probably wouldn't have had that either. So you can see as to where I kind of had to step up."

"No not really," Doctor Susan said, "you did have a choice. You could have walked away and taken the chance of him losing everything, and that's what most people would have done. But you, you didn't; you took it on. And it takes a strong person with a lot of character to take on that kind of responsibility. You obviously care a great deal about him."

"More than most people would ever know," Mark somberly replied, "but trust me, I didn't do it alone. If it wasn't for my wife, and a few, and I say few, supportive family members; especially lately, I probably would have ended up in an asylum or something comparable."

"Yeah Mark, that all may be true. But you're the one that took it all on, and like I said before, it really takes a person with strength and character to do all of what you did for him."

"Yeah I know it does, and I know I did the right thing, but there's a part of me that doesn't feel like I did."

Puzzled, Doctor Susan asked, "Why?"

Mark replied, "Well to start with, my uncle makes me feel that way. I won't even go and see him anymore because of it. And then the state workers, and the fucking lawyers really don't make me feel that way."

"Go on."

"Well you see, three weeks ago, I got a letter stating that the home John has been in for almost a year now, is closing. One of the reasons why is because Medicaid will no longer pay for patients to stay there. What the other reasons are I have no clue. So yeah, okay, cool, I thought. John's gonna get his wish, he's gonna be moved to a different place; preferably one that's closer. He'd been complaining about wanting to be moved for quite some time. I'd been trying to get him moved myself, but my hands were tied, even though I had gotten his insurance straightened out, I had no luck. Every place I tried was full; I could never get that through his head though. He would literally throw temper tantrums when I tried to tell him he had to wait. Personally, even though the home he was in was a ways away and wasn't exactly the nicest place to be in, I thought he was in really good hands. And he was also where he needed to be. Hell, they got him off from the feeding tube and back on solid food again, so they had to be good. He didn't think so though; all he did was complain, scream and yell, and throw fits, and I know damn well no matter what place he was in he was gonna act that way. No one could tell him anything, and I know the dementia was part of the reason for his behavior, and it was probably really tough for him, but man let me tell you, it could get, and was downright frustrating. There were times I just wanted to fucking strangle him, that's why I stopped going to see him..." Mark paused for a moment, cleared his throat, and said, "Once I signed him into the place he was moved to, and I got everything there straight, I made up my mind. I would take care of his finances and deal with his doctors and nurses, but I totally refused to see him anymore. It just became too heart-wrenching and downright aggravating, especially during the two or three weeks before he was moved. My god man, for me, and I really don't know why, but everything, including just day-to-day functioning became a mental nightmare. I felt so sick all the time, and sort of still do."

"Why Mark? What happened?"

"Well, I started getting phone calls from so many different state agencies that it wasn't funny. One wanted to know what I was doing with John's SSI check, because John had said I was stealing it. There was a huge bill owed to the prior home he was in, which I never received, but I did pay when I found out about it. And I never stole a single dime from him. I'm still clueless as to why he said that.... Hmm, he even told them I sold his car and kept the money from it, which was a lie. I did get rid of it though; the thing was such a piece of junk that it was a death trap. So I had a junk yard come and get it, and I told him when he got home we would get him a new one, which he agreed to. But because of his driving record, he's not allowed to register a car in the state of Michigan anyways. So that really wasn't gonna happen."

"Why's that? Too many tickets?" Doctor Susan asked as she uncrossed her legs and sat up straight.

"No, too many drunk drivings." Mark replied, "John's on the, "Three strikes, you're out," deal, which he also has outstanding warrants for."

"Really, why?"

"Because he never showed up to court for one of the fines, which I also had to inform the F.I.A. workers about…. Hmm, he also told them I ran off with a large sum of his money, which was a lie. After my wife and I caught all of his back bills up and set aside a funeral fund for him, we used the rest of his money to clean and fix up his home…. You know, just in case he got to go home. Well that, and because the township threatened to condemn it, which I also had to explain to the state workers, and the fucking lawyers. Man, it's a good thing I saved every single receipt and stub from everything we had done. There's no telling what might have happened if I didn't, and John also threw a fit about that. He said," "You had no right doing that, there was nothing wrong with my trailer!" "Man, to him I didn't have a right to do shit; fucking asshole! For some reason, and I try to keep telling myself that it was due to the dementia, and in his twisted state of mind he really thought there wasn't anything wrong with his home and the way he'd been living;

we all knew better, but no one was going to tell him any different. You know, he even almost had the state workers convinced he was ready to go back to his home….." Mark paused for a moment again, and said, "It's a good thing it still wouldn't pass inspection, because I really think they would have let him, regardless of my approval. And that would have been fucked up, and every new thing in the trailer within a week or two would have been fucked up as well. Why they were even considering it, was way beyond me. They said something about home health care. Yeah, right! Kara and I knew there was no way that was gonna work. He would have ended up throwing them out, and the whole ordeal would have just started all over again. Besides, the man had dementia; they shouldn't have even been discussing it with him."

"That's true."

"You know I was even threatened with prison." Mark said with anger.

"Really?"

"Oh yeah, right up until the day John was moved I was still being accused of stealing his SSI. I even had a few aunts accusing me of it. Which was an outright lie; I never misused any of his money."

"But you could prove that, right?"

"Oh yeah, I could definitely prove I wasn't stealing from him, and I knew I could. But even though I knew and still know, it weighed heavily on my mind, and still somewhat does."

"Why's that Mark? I mean if you could and can prove it, then why worry?"

"Well, because I didn't want someone showing up at my

door and interrupting my and Kara's quiet life with some kind of stupid investigation. Our lives had already been interrupted enough, and besides, you know as well as I do, even when you know you've done nothing wrong, and you can prove it. Some people in certain positions, if they really want to, can and will make it look like you've done something wrong. And if you don't believe that, well take a look at all the innocent people throughout history that have been wrongly persecuted."

"No, I agree with you, you're right, and that's all true. But I'm sensing that you may have some un-resolved issues. Issues that cause you at times to be just slightly paranoid. Do you think so?"

"Oh I know so," Mark replied, "and with some things yes. Well, probably a lot of things. I feel I've mainly by society, been conditioned to feel that way. Especially when it comes to mine and my wife's livelihood, I get real paranoid, or defensive, or whatever you want to call it. I mean come on, everywhere you go, or look, there's some kind of message on some sign or billboard, or advertisement, or just a piece of paper or something with some kind of jail, prison, or a ridiculous punishment threat on it. It seems to me as though our society, or just humans in general thrive on that type of shit, and it annoys the hell out of me. Especially when I'm the one being directly threatened. You know yourself that you can't go anywhere without seeing that type of thing… Hmm, I bet I could find something in this room with some kind of threat on it."

"That's true. But why take notice?" Doctor Susan asked with deep curiosity; she really couldn't grasp why he felt the way he did, and she really wanted to get deep into his mind.

"Well when something is constantly in your face," Mark

replied with passion, "it's hard not to. And when you see good, honest people everywhere and every day going down for something stupid, or downright ridiculous, like I said before, when it's directed at you, you can have just cause to be a little paranoid."

"But if you're not doing anything wrong, why worry?" Doctor Susan sternly asked.

Mark snapped back at her with somewhat of an evil sounding snarl, "You've obviously never been accused of doing something you didn't do!"

This shocked her, and rather than say, "You obviously have," like she wanted too, and she now knew he had been. Doctor Susan just humbly replied, "Good point," cleared her throat, and quickly changed the pace with, "Do you ever have any real strong feelings of paranoia, you know, things such as someone is out to get you? Someone's watching me, my wife's having an affair, etc, things like that?"

"No, never." Mark replied with a much calmer sounding tone.

"Okay, good. Now, did the feelings of anxiety or paranoia continue after your uncle was moved?"

"No not really, I mean I still every once in a while find myself reflecting on the whole thing, and getting mad about it. And I do sometimes think there still could be some kind of investigation. But in reality, it's unlikely that will ever happen. Because when I proved to all those dick head dumb asses that I had power of attorney over him and his estate, they left me alone. At least I think they did?"

"What do you mean?"

"Well after he was moved I had my number changed, no,

actually I had the house phone shut off and I got a cell phone. Man, if I had to hear that house phone ring any more than it had I was gonna go nuts. You know I argued over that phone with so many different people so many different times, I would actually have tremors when I heard it ring. So it's gone, and if they're still calling, I wouldn't know, and I don't wanna know. But now the problem is every time something happens with him at the home he's in now, they always call my cell phone, and I then immediately go on the defense and think, *Oh boy, here we go again,* and the nervousness and the panic attacks start all over again."

"What do these calls usually involve? Are you still being accused of wrongdoing?" Doctor Susan asked.

"No," Mark replied while he moved around as if he was uncomfortable, "now it's always over John being how John's going to be until he's no longer of this earth."

Mark found a comfortable position…

Doctor Susan asked, "And how is he being, Mark?"

"Well he's being real combative with the staff, he's refusing his meds, he's claiming he's not a diabetic, he's climbed out of bed several times and knocked his TV to the floor, he tried to strangle himself. And when he found out I sold his trailer he threw a total fit, which really confused me because he had agreed that we'd sell it, and when he got even better he would live in an assisted living community, which is what he said he wanted. But man, the way he acts now I don't think that's ever gonna happen."

"No Mark, it's probably not. The harsh reality is, because of his dementia, which from the sounds of it has progressed, he's going to have to remain where he is. And that's probably the best place for him."

"Yeah I know that. But I can still wish, can't I?"

"Yes, you sure can," Doctor Susan replied with a smile, "So keep wishing, and don't give up hope either. But don't let it completely drive you. Because if you do, you're only setting yourself up for bigger disappointment, and that could lead you to deeper symptoms of anxiety and depression. Try to find a happy medium."

"Yeah that's true…. Hmm," Mark paused for a moment, "should I feel bad for refusing to go and see him?"

"No not at all. You're taking care of his business, and dealing with his doctors, and if seeing him drains you too much, then no, don't see him, and don't feel bad about it. You have to have time for you as well, plus remember, he's in the hands of trained professionals. So try not to worry too much.."

"I'm trying not to."

"Good, that's a very healthy choice…. Now has any of this affected your relationship with your wife in any negative way?"

"No not really, we get along great, we don't really have any fights, and truthfully I'd like to think we have almost the picture-perfect marriage, which I'm very grateful for."

"Well that's good. Most of us, if not all of us, could only dream of feeling that way. You're very lucky."

"Yeah I know I am. Kara has been so wonderful, especially through this whole ordeal. She's been so supportive, most people, including myself would have walked away a long time ago. Not her though; she's been sticking it out with me…. She's also actually one of the main reasons I'm here."

"Really? Why is that?"

"Well when she had noticed what was going on with my

emotions, she suggested that maybe seeking some kind of counseling would help."

"Is it?"

"Yeah, it's somewhat helping. It's just not helping as fast as I would like it too."

"Well as you know, this is gonna take some time. But, you'll find that if you stick it out, and if you really want them to, these sessions will work."

"Oh believe me I want them to, and I'm going to keep using the methods you suggested."

"Good," Doctor Susan replied with a smile. She also took a quick look at her watch, Mark caught the hint, and she carried on, "Also if you want, try to get on some kind of workout program. You'll find that exercise will raise your dopamine levels and help lower your stress levels."

"Yeah, you know I've read about that. And you know what, I think I'll give it a try."

"Good. Now if you wouldn't mind? I'd like for just your wife to come in next session, and then the following session I would like to see you both at the same time. Is that all right?"

"Yeah, that sounds good to me."

"Okay great. Then I'll see you in two weeks, and your wife in a week. If you need anything beforehand or have any questions, please feel free to call me or my hotline."

"I'll do that, and thanks."

"You bet."

Mark left the office and went home…

Doctor Susan followed him out to the waiting room and called in her next patient…

7

Session Four

Shortly after Mark got home from his session with Doctor Susan, he told Kara how it went, and how he was now feeling about things. He also told her about Doctor Susan wanting to see her, and then the both of them together, which Kara agreed to do. So when a week went by, and it was time for her to go to her scheduled appointment, she went. But shortly after she arrived, Kara soon found out that her appointment had been abruptly canceled. Puzzled as to why she wasn't notified sooner, Kara politely asked one of the office assistants why, and what the reason for the cancellation was.

She was simply told, "We're sorry, but Doctor Susan had a sudden emergency that she had to attend to. Would you like to schedule another appointment?"

"Um, no." Kara replied and said, "I think there's already one scheduled for next week."

"Would you like me to check?"

"Sure if you don't mind?"

"Nope, not at all." The assistant replied, and said as she rapidly typed a few keys on her computer keyboard, "Just one moment."

Staring at the computer screen in front of her, the office assistant quickly looked through a few electronic files, and said, "Yep, there's an appointment here for two p.m. one week from today. Sound good?"

"Yep, it sure does." Kara replied with a smile.

"Okay then, we'll see you in a week, and we're terribly sorry for the inconvenience. If we would have known sooner we would have called."

"That's alright," Kara replied and said with a wide smile, "these kind of things happen, plus I probably needed to get out anyway. Have a good day."

"You too, and thanks for being so understanding."

"No problem."

8

Driving home from Doctor Susan's office, Kara casually made her way through the streets of the small township where she and Mark lived. Humming along to a mellow tune that played softly through the car's stereo system, Kara thought about what she was going to do with the rest of her day. She also thought and tried to decide on what to make for dinner that evening.

"Oh I know." She spoke out loud, "I'll make spaghetti, it's been awhile since we've had it, plus it's Mark's favorite. Now that I'm eating for two though, I'd better make a little extra." *Hmm, I wonder?* she then thought, *Do we even have the stuff at home to make it? I think we do, but just in case we don't, I had better stop at the store, or I could just call Mark and see. Naw, I'll stop and get everything.*

Stopping at a traffic signal and still mentally making her plans, Kara's thoughts turned to the sound of the car's stereo.

Her ears tuned in sharply to the local news...

Hearing the weather forecast and a few other minute things, Kara sort of sat in shock at the next thing she heard:

"A Prominent local Heart Surgeon, named Richard Downs, who was a major part of the Local Hospitals and Doctor's offices Health Systems, was just recently found only a few hours ago outside of his office dead in his car..."

Doctor Susan's husband? Kara thought as the traffic light turned green and she drove away. *No way... Wow! That must have been what the emergency was all about. That poor woman, man... Wait till Mark hears about it...*

9

Session Five

Sitting and patiently waiting in Doctor Susan's office, not sure of what to do or say, and also surprised it hadn't been canceled. One week later, Mark went to the appointment that had been scheduled for him and Kara by himself. Looking around the room while he sat, Mark thought about the events in his, Kara's and Doctor Susan's lives that had just recently taken place. Not too sure if it was really Doctor Susan's husband that was found dead one week ago, Mark made a point to himself not to ask her if it was. Still though, he was quite curious to know if it was indeed her husband. *But, Mark thought, if it was, I highly doubt she'd already be back to work. But still, maybe it was.. Who knows? She'll probably say something if it was… But I'm not gonna bring it up.*

Mark then had a complete moment of mental silence…

For the first time, in which sometimes to him felt like an eternity, Mark's mind was totally silent and at rest. It felt good.

Doctor Susan stepped into the room, closed the door behind her, sat in her chair, smiled at Mark, and said, "Hello. How are we doing today?"

"Good."

"That's good. How's things going with your high levels of anxiety? Any major problems?"

"No, not really." Mark replied.

"Have the methods I suggested for you to use when things get hard been helping?"

"Yeah sort of, but in the past week I've became so busy that I really didn't have time to use them. Shit! I really didn't even have much time to think, and I think that was part of my problem."

"Maybe, but carry on. What kept you so busy?" Doctor Susan asked as she sat back.

"Well as sad as it was and is, five days ago my uncle died. He aspirated and asphyxiated before anyone at the home could get to him."

"Oh wow, I'm so sorry to hear that." Doctor Susan said with concern as she leaned back up.

"Yeah me too…" Mark somberly replied.

"How have you been taking it?"

"Well I immediately took care of his funeral arrangements and closed out his estate, um so, I guess you could say I've been taking it very well. I mean I have my moments of sadness and confusion, but for the most part I've been holding up very well."

"And your wife, how's she been taking it?"

"She's been taking it well. She's shared some of my sadness and helped me carry the burden, so I guess she's doing good."

"That's good. Um, if you don't mind me asking, because I can't remember if I asked you or not. How old was he?"

"He was sixty-three."

"Yeah okay, sixty-three. That's what I thought, I just couldn't remember if I had already asked you that or not. Sorry.."

"No, that's cool."

"Any overwhelming feelings over his death, you know;

feeling like you can't go on, or anything comparable?"

"No not really," Mark replied, "now I'm just having what I call long moments of peaceful silence."

"Well that's good." Doctor Susan said as she leaned back again. She could tell Mark was a lot more at ease then he had been in the other sessions, and this made her feel safe and at ease as well. She still sensed he was hiding something though, and she wanted badly to know what it was.

Mark said, "You know, I know that this may not sound right, but part of me feels somewhat relieved, and not just for myself. I kind of feel that way for him as well. I mean that man was suffering, and if he wasn't going to get better he had needed to go. Why he or we had to go through everything we did, I'll never comprehend, because it all totally sucked. No one should have to go through any of that shit, but we did, and like I said before, a big part of me feels relieved. Is that normal?"

"Yes," Doctor Susan replied, "it's perfectly normal to feel that way, especially when things had been carrying on for you, him, and your wife for so long… And it's very understandable. I noticed though, you said, "Somewhat relieved." When you say, "Somewhat," that tells me you may still have some unclear feelings, which is also understandable. It's going to take some time for you to work through all of your feelings, and honestly, for some it can take almost a lifetime. In your case though, I don't see that happening, and we won't let it. So, could you tell me what, "Somewhat," is all about?"

"Well I say somewhat relieved because, every now and then, even though John's gone and his estate is closed, and everything that was his is gone, because I gave it all away and used his remaining money to bury him and pay the rest of his bills. I still think something concerning something to do with him is gonna creep up."

"Why do you feel that way, Mark?"

"Because you know as well as I do, with the human race something always comes up. Even though for me, except for a slow mourning period, it's all over. For someone else though, it's probably not, and that's all the fuel that someone needs to start something."

"Something like what?"

"Something like an unpaid bill or screwed-up paperwork, that always happens, and someone usually has to pitch a bitch about it."

"True," Doctor Susan Said, "but you said for you, except for the slow mourning period, that it's over."

"It is." Mark replied as he leaned back.

"Well then if you really feel that way, even if someone starts something up again, no matter what it is, you need to keep telling yourself that. And them. And you are right, people do have a bad way of rekindling things, but sometimes if you just simply walk away and don't feed the fire, the fire won't be built."

"That's true, but for a short while I'm probably not gonna feel that way."

"Yes, but in time you should."

"Yeah as long as nothing creeps up I will."

"Even if it does, so what? Walk away and realize that this is your time. Someone that you obviously held dear to you has passed on, and no one, and I mean no one has the right to bring you lower. Bring yourself up and reflect on the good memories you have of him. But don't live in them, and definitely don't let anyone make you feel like you did things wrong, or make you feel like you owe, because you don't."

"Oh trust me," Mark replied with a sigh, "that's what I've been doing, and is what I'm gonna keep doing."

"Good, and you'll find if that's the way you truly want it, then that's the way you'll have it. The peaceful moments should also start overriding the un-peaceful ones as well."

"Oh they are."

"Good. Now tell me what your relationship with John was like before he fell ill."

Mark sat forward and said, "Well from the time I was really young, he was always in my life. Then he was more like a father figure than an uncle, probably because my dad was never really around. Dad was more worried about getting drunk and getting his dick wet then being there for me." Doctor Susan snickered at Mark's remark, and he also laughed for a moment, and then kept talking, "That was okay with me though, because I didn't even really like the guy."

"Really?" Doctor Susan asked with surprise.

"Yeah, that's true. In fact, I could never see what my mother saw in him, and I still don't."

"Wow! That's harsh!"

"Maybe." Mark replied, "Anyways, my dad's a whole different story….. I did everything with John, especially when I got older, and then he became more like a best friend; we did almost anything you could imagine. Hmm, we even did things that people shouldn't; things that I'll take to my grave. I loved him. Sometimes I think his influence on my life is what inspired my passion for writing stories."

"Why's that?"

"Well when I was four or five, I think. It's really foggy now…. Anyways I was young. I used to go with him every once in a while to his place of work. He worked at some kind of large retail store chain back then, it's long been closed down now, and I would always eyeball this little kid's record player. Do you remember them? They were usually made out of plastic, and they had a lid and a handle that would close it up so you could carry it places."

"Yeah I remember those. They would play forty-fives and thirty-threes, plus they usually sounded terrible."

"Yeah they sure did, but the story records you could get for them usually sounded pretty good."

"That's true. Go on."

"Well just to make a long story short, John bought the player I had been eyeballing and gave it to me for Christmas that year. I thought it was the coolest thing, and I still do, and man, over the next five years I used that thing so much the motor in it eventually burned up. I sat at that player for, man. I couldn't count how many hours, and I would listen to story after story. And music; John had given me a bunch of records with just music on them. I couldn't tell you who the bands were now, but I swear I wore them all out. You know, to this day I'm still so surprised it never drove my mother nuts, which was a good thing."

"Yeah, that would be a good thing." Doctor Susan said with a smile.

Mark replied, "Yeah it was. You know, one time my mother and I moved into this trailer, I think I was six. Wow, that was along time ago… Anyways, the day we were setting my bedroom up, I found a little rack of forty-fives sitting in the closet. Someone had obviously left them behind, so they were mine, and boy did they get their use. I still can't figure out what happened to them though. We moved so much when I was young, things constantly got misplaced. The record player never did though, up until the day it stopped working I always knew where it was, and I always knew where John was."

"It sounds like your uncle helped create some good memories for you."

"Yeah he did, and I'm sure he had some of his own. For most of my life he was a very special person to me, and I'd like to think I was special to him. But when he started to get sick and fell ill, I began having my doubts. I think because I was so close to him at one time is why everything hurt so much. Especially when he started accusing me of stealing from him. That actually hurt the most."

"I can understand that," Doctor Susan said, "and I think most people would have been hurt. Also your hurt is normal, but to help make that hurt go away, you have to remember and keep telling yourself he was sick. The dementia he had caused him to do the things and say the things he did. It wasn't anything you did or did wrong."

"Yeah I know," Mark replied, "and I've slowly been convincing myself of that. Its just when you loved someone wholeheartedly your whole life, it's hard. You know the day of his funeral, when I watched his casket lower into the ground, I felt such a feeling of peace… I didn't cry, I did my crying two days prior, I didn't laugh. Hmm… I didn't feel really anything but an inner peace, and that peace; it felt so warm. So warm that it was like something was holding me from the inside and saying to me, "It's okay now, now move forward and live." I was also glad it was over with. Isn't that strange?"

"No not really, I just recently experienced the same thing."

"Really, what happened?"

"My husband died two weeks ago. He was found in his car outside of his office. He supposedly had a massive heart attack, and I just buried him four days ago."

"Wow... Sorry to hear that," Mark said, and also thought at the same time, *So, it was her husband.*

"Yeah me too," Doctor Susan replied with a half-smile, "and thanks."

"Yeah sure, no problem. Um... So if you don't mind me asking?"

"No, go ahead."

"Was your husband the heart surgeon, Richard Downs; the one the local news kept talking about?"

"Yep, he sure was."

"Wow... Again I'm sorry... Kara and I thought he might have been, but we didn't wanna ask."

"No... That's okay. Being the well-known-man he was, and sharing the same last name, I've been asked that question more times then I can count, especially lately, so you wouldn't have been the first, and I take no offense. I actually find it welcoming."

"How so?" Mark asked.

"Well..." Doctor Susan politely replied, "It reminds me that I was married to a well-known-man who touched a lot of people in a positive way, and it also makes me feel privileged to have had the time spent with him. Even though it wasn't long, it was very wonderful, and I'll hold that feeling with me the rest of my life."

"Wow... That's what I call holding up well."

"Oh trust me, I've had my moments... And I'll probably have a few more. But for now, that's how I feel, and I hope to keep it that way... Now as for you, along with using the methods I told you to use to combat your anxiety and depression when it kicks in, also try to think of all the good memories that you shared with your uncle. You'll find that should also help."

"Oh trust me, since he died that's what I've been doing, and it seems to be working."

"Good... Have the feelings of anxiousness or depression been overwhelming, or have you had any symptoms?"

"No not really... Now I spend a lot of time reflecting."

"Do you feel these sessions have helped you in any way?" Doctor Susan asked as she looked at her watch like she always did.

Mark caught the usual hint, and replied, "Oh yeah, definitely... The methods you suggested have been like little miracles."

"Good... Now do you think you need more sessions, or do you think you're alright with everything and I can close your case?"

"Hmm, you know, I'm not really sure."

"Okay then, if you're not sure... I'll tell you what I'm going to do, I'll go ahead and leave your case open and let you decide. I won't schedule you another session, but if you feel you need more, you can give me or my office a call and come back without starting over. Sound good to you?"

"Yeah that sounds great, and thanks."

"You bet. Good luck, and enjoy the rest of your day."

"You too."

10

Driving home from his appointment that afternoon, Mark felt refreshed, and for the first time to him in what seemed like an eternity, he felt good about everything. Nothing felt wrong, and everything felt right. He also couldn't wait to get home to see Kara. She had an obstetrician appointment that day, so Mark was excited; he really wanted to hear how it went, *Good*, he hoped; *with everything that had recently taken place good news would be a very welcoming thing.*

His car's phone then rang through it's audio system.

Pressing a button on the steering wheel, Mark said, "Yeah, hello."

"Mark?"

"Yeah, who's this and what can I do for you?"

"This is Andrea, I'm a publicist for J and D publishing. How you doing?'

"Good. How about you?"

"Not bad."

"Good, glad to hear it. You know I think we've spoken before?"

"Yeah we probably have. Probably more than once."

"Yeah probably. Anyways, Andrea, what can I do for you?"

"Well first of all, I would like to congratulate you on your book titled "Far off And Running's," climbing to number one in such a short amount of time. That's quite impressive, especially in this business."

"Well thank you."

"You're very welcome, and I would also like to add that I personally loved the book. I think it's a brilliant masterpiece that will surely stand the test of time."

"Gee thanks, I don't think I've ever heard it put that way."

"Again, you're welcome. I could carry on about it for hours! Ha, ha ha. But I can't do that right now, so I'd better get on with it. Two weeks from now, our company and others like us are holding a large book convention at a well-known gateway center just shortly north of you, and we would like you to attend, and represent us as our star author of the year. And also sign some books. Would you be interested in doing this for us, and yourself?"

"Oh yeah, it would be an honor."

"So you can commit?"

"Yep, I'll be there."

"Good then, in a few hours I'll email you all the info on the convention and everything you'll need to know. Sound good?"

"Yeah that sounds great. One thing though?"

"What's that?"

"Will I need to bring my own books?"

"Nope; we're supplying everything you'll need."

"Even lunch?" Laughed Mark.

"Yes Mark, even lunch. Well that's if you still have the same email address so I can send you the info?"

"Yeah I still have the same address, and It's in your system right?"

"Yep, it sure is."

"Okay then, I'll be watching for it."

"Okay, and I'm looking forward to seeing you there."

"You too, and have a good day."

"You as well. Bye now, and I'll be seeing you."

"K, bye… Hot fucking damn!" Mark then yelled as he tapped a hang up button with his thumb. "Things are definitely starting to go in the right direction. I can't wait to tell Kara about this. Uncle John, wherever you are, thanks for looking over me. Man, I'm gonna have to call my mom and tell her about this. I'll wait till I get home though. She's gonna be so excited, and so is Kara."

Rolling the car's window all the way down, and cranking up the stereo, Mark yelled as loud as he could while he hurried home, "Whew!"

11

Two weeks later, and after days and days of better and better news, the day of the big book convention came, and Mark was feeling so good about it, and everything else in his life that came with it, that his whole mental being was just a flood of warm feeling emotion; which also included the fact that Kara's obstetrician appointment two-weeks prior went well. Plus the fact that they were gonna have a girl. Ever since Mark was a little boy he dreamed of having a little girl by his side. He never really knew why he did; he just did. It was one of those things that couldn't be explained. The dream and the feelings were just there, and now the dream was going to come true. What a wonderful feeling for Mark, and Kara as well, was to know that his book career was obviously going to take off. The woman of his dreams was carrying the child that he had always wanted, and he felt he no longer needed Doctor Susan's assistance. He could now move forward and leave all the bad behind, and that's exactly what he did, and planned on doing for the rest of his life.

The day before the convention, Mark even went to his uncle's place of burial and said his final good byes. He told him thanks for everything he had done for him, and how grateful he was for the influence John had on his life. It was now done. Mark wept a small tear of joy; the hardship for them both was over. But there was a part of Mark that still wished John could be there, and things could be like they were when they were young. Mark knew that it was impossible though, he knew it was time to move on; move on to the new and exciting path that now seemed to lay before him. Anything was possible, the sky was the limit, and Mark was ready for it. In fact, Mark felt as though he was ready for just about anything, and he was.

Over the past few days Mark experienced such an inner sense of self renewal, that he felt like a completely different person. He looked forward to things; he didn't feel nervous and alone, he didn't feel he had to shy away from people. There wasn't a single feeling of hate in his body, and at the book convention it really showed. Mark, with his beautiful glowing, pregnant wife by his side; who looked really ravishing that day, and also dripped with feminine beauty, shook hands with all sorts of different people. People from all different walks of life and professions flocked to the convention and made their way around the large Gateway Center. There were authors, publishers, movie agents, fans, literary agents, simple patrons, salespeople, C.E.O.S, college students, kids with their mothers and fathers, teachers, doctors, lawyers and laymen. When any one of them approached the spot Mark's company had set up for him and asked for a signed copy of one of his books, he tingled with excitement and gladly signed. He felt honored, and with each book he signed and sold, Mark's positive outlook on things grew and grew. He felt he knew what his purpose in life finally was... He loved every minute of it, and he also loved sharing it all with Kara; who he loved and adored so much that he would have given his life for if the situation arrived. He was so grateful for having her in his life. A large part of him felt as though if it hadn't been for her and her unconditional love for him, and life itself, that he would have never made it through the ordeal with his uncle. He loved her so much, and as the day went along, every once in a while Mark would think, *I'm going to do something nice for her. For all the support that woman has given me, she deserves it, and I kind of owe it to her. What a lucky man I' am, any other woman would have walked away from me along time ago. She didn't though, and for that I'm extremely grateful. I just haven't told her yet. But I'm going to, after this little shindig is over I'm gonna let her know... Maybe I'll take her on vacation? Yeah that's what I'll do... Hmm... We can go to the cottage, and then maybe the U.P. or something. She'd really enjoy that... Me too... Kind of like how I'm enjoying this... Man there's a lot of people here, and man I've signed and sold a lot of books. It's turning out to be a pretty good day... I hope like hell I get to do more of these things... Don't see why not? Hey is that...?* Mark then thought as he spotted a familiar face in the crowd, *No it can't be!*

Turning his full attention to the familiar face, Mark mumbled to himself, "It is... What the hell is she doing here?"

Kara was sitting next to Mark. She giggled and asked, "What's that Mark? Why are you talking to yourself?"

A few people lined up at the table that sat in front of the both of them, Mark leaned over to Kara and whispered in her ear, "I'll tell you later."

He leaned back and turned his attention to each and every individual that approached him.

Signing each person's book, and quickly speaking with them as they passed by, Mark gratefully and heart-fully did his duty as a writer and representative to his company.

He also had fun with it...

He laughed, he joked, he introduced Kara, and he was also surprised a few times at what people had to say. He was especially surprised when the person he had recognized a moment earlier in the crowd got into the line, quickly stepped up to his table, and happily said, "Hey Mark. How you doing?"

"Um… Doctor Susan hi, I um. I'm doing good. Yourself?"

"Good. As a matter of fact I'm doing really well, thanks for asking. Now are you going to introduce me, or do I have to introduce myself?"

"Huh, what do you? Oh yeah, I'm sorry. Kara, this is Doctor Susan; Doctor Susan, this is my wife Kara."

Holding out her hand and shaking Doctor Susan's, Kara smiled and said, "Wow, I've heard so much about you that it's nice to have finally met you."

"Likewise." Doctor Susan replied with a warm smile.

She broke away from the handshake and said to Mark as she handed him a book, "So, you gonna sign this for me? Or do I have to arm wrestle you for it?"

Laughing while Kara laughed as well, Mark replied, "Well, since you put it that way, I'd better sign it."

Opening the book, he quickly signed the inside insert with his name, and a few words that simply said, *"To Doctor Susan. Thank you very much for all of your support, your friend. Mark…"*

He handed the book back to Doctor Susan and asked, "So what brings you up and out this way anyway? You're not stalking me are you?"

Doctor Susan laughed, as did Kara. She replied, "I knew you were gonna ask me that, so no… I'm not stalking you."

"Yeah just kidding. I know you're not."

"Well since you put it that way, maybe I am."

The three of them all then laughed.

Doctor Susan continued with, "No really, I'm not. One of my colleagues is here promoting a book she wrote on the different stages of porn and sex addiction, and I came to give her some support."

"Really? Wow, that's cool. Maybe later we'll stop by her booth and check out her book."

"Yeah, that sounds nice. Plus she would probably really appreciate that, and she's also a fan of your books. So in fact, I know she would."

"Wow that's even better. Um if you don't mind me asking...?"

"Nope, not at all."

"How did you know I was here?"

"Mark, please. Your name and face are both on the banner at the front of the building."

Laughing as Kara laughed as well, Mark replied, "Oh yeah, that's right. I forgot about that."

"Yeah silly. Anyways by the looks of the line, I'd better get out of here and let you do your job. Kara, nice meeting you."

"Thanks, you too."

"And Mark, congrats and good luck."

"Okay, and thanks again for the support."

"You bet, and we'll see you."

Doctor Susan then walked off while Mark turned to Kara and said, "Wow, that was weird."

"Why's that?"

"I don't know? It just was."

"Okay, if you say so. I thought it was sweet, and I also think she has a thing for you."

"Oh please...?"

Kara giggled and said, "Oh yeah, by the gleam she had in her eyes, I'd say it's a pretty big thing."

Kara giggled again while Mark laughed and said, "Stop, you're freaking me out."

He went back to signing books while Kara leaned to him and whispered in his ear, "She wants you baaaaaaaad, big boy."

Mark replied, "Stop…"

Kara leaned back and giggled again.

Mark just shook his head, grinned a silly grin, and happily greeted the next person in line.

Pleasantly signing their book, and each and every one that others wanted signed, Mark kicked back, relaxed, and enjoyed the rest of the day.

As it carried on and seemed to quickly fly by, with a deep feeling of accomplishment and satisfaction, Mark and Kara soon found themselves reaching the end of the convention.

Mark especially felt satisfied, which is something he hadn't felt in a long time. For him, and Kara as well, it was a really good feeling. It was such a good feeling that they planned on going out and celebrating after they got home.

They really felt that way when he and Kara were preparing to leave and Andrea, who'd been all day at a separate booth doing the selling of Mark's books, came to them and told them that all of the books the publisher had provided that day had sold out. And Mark's books were the only ones that did. That made them both feel really warm on the inside. They were so excited, and now they were really going to celebrate.

Three days later while at home and working on the book that Doctor Susan had inspired him to write, Mark got a phone call from his publisher. It was Andrea again, and she had called to inform him that he and Kara were invited by a group of publishers and agents to a big dinner banquet in New York

City. This was all being covered by his publisher; Mark and Kara didn't have to pay any of the expenses, it was all on them.

Wow! What an honor! Mark thought.

So a few days later, they went, and they both had a wonderful, romantic time. It seemed as though after everything they had went through, that they were falling deeper in love with each other, and in a way what had happened had brought them closer together. Mark loved Kara so much, and she loved him equally as well; all things were good.

12

A few days after they had gone to the dinner banquet in New York City, Mark and Kara arrived home and immediately went on vacation like Mark had planned. For three weeks the two of them stayed gone, just doing whatever their hearts desired together. There was no work, no phones, no computers, no hustle and bustle of everyday life, and the both of them loved every minute of it.

They also loved each other very much, and they also loved Northern Michigan almost as much, but not quite as much as they loved each other. So that's where they went; they went to Northern Michigan and spent the first leg of their vacation touring the Upper Peninsula.

First they visited numerous historical sites, and took various tours of all different kinds of museums, which was something they had done before, but neither one of them cared because it was something they had both loved to do. They especially loved doing it together, and they loved doing it worry-free, which was also something the both of them had needed for a long time, and was very well-deserved. For the both of them it felt good, it was so relaxing and stress-free, that if they'd had it their way, they would never go back; they'd stay there for good. But the both of them knew at the moment that was kind of impossible. Someday they would though, maybe once a little more money from Mark's books rolled in. Even though at the time, they were doing financially well, they both knew at the moment it would probably take a little more then they had. Plus with a baby on the way they wouldn't be able to do, or find the time to do the remodeling job that would need to be done to their cottage on Thunder Bay. Remodeling would be necessary to make the cottage comfortable for the three of them. They would then just sell their house and live there. But for now they would have to wait and see how things were going to go.

At least they had the cottage though, that's what really mattered the most to them. It was a place that neither one of them ever wanted to lose, and after they finished traveling around the U.P. for about a week and a half, that's where they spent the rest of their vacation. They spent it at their cozy little three-room cottage that sat on the southern shores of the beautiful and somewhat mystical Thunder Bay.

What a magical place that was, and still is, and to them it was somewhat of a heavenly place to be. The view of Lake Huron from the back side of the cottage was in a way breathtaking, and the energy that surrounded it and the whole general area was very soothing. It had almost a other worldly sense to it, and at times, to some, it could be very intoxicating. This was only one of the many reasons why a couple of years ago when the place had went up for sale, Mark and Kara decided to buy it, and make it their little getaway place.

And get away they did. Every time they went there they always had a wonderful, and quite romantic time. Being there for them was like living in total bliss. Every morning after breakfast they would go for a long walk. In the afternoon after lunch, they would spend most of that time lounging on the beach, playing around in the lake, or they would just simply take long rides on their two-person, personal watercraft.

They also went for long bike rides through the wooded trails that were within close vicinity to the cottage.

At night, usually after dinner, they would always have a small beach fire. That's when they would do a lot of heartfelt talking, planning for the coming baby, and reminiscing.

That's also when Mark had finally thanked Kara for everything.

One night under the star-filled sky, a cool mid-September breeze began to mildly blow across the calm waters of Thunder Bay, and as it did, it gently came to shore and rolled along the soft, pale moonlit sand. Mark and Kara sat in nice outdoor folding chairs around a small fire that he had just built. The light coming from the inside of the cottage was ghostly dim. The sound of low mellow music softly hummed from the distance as it traveled from somewhere and everywhere through an open window. The fire softly crackled with the sounds of burning embers, and the light smell of smoke and pine surrounded the area. The low yellow-orange light that the fire created softly and dimly lit part of their surroundings with a warm sensuous glow.

Mark, in deep thought, stared into the fire for a moment and said to Kara as he looked her in the eyes, and momentarily admired her warmly lit, and also very beautiful face, "I wanna thank you for everything."

"Thank me for what Mark?"

"You know, everything in the past two years that you've helped me with. I want to thank you for all of it. I don't think if you would have been in my life I would have made it through all that shit we went through. And I also want to say I'm sorry for not saying thanks a lot sooner. And I really love you for all of it."

"Wow that's really sweet Mark, but you don't have to thank me or apologize. I'm your wife. I love you, and that's what I'm here for."

"I know, but I want to thank you anyways; it's the least I could do. I'd been planning on telling you for a while, I just wanted to wait for the right time, and right now feels like the right time. So…" Mark continued with as he got up from his chair, took Kara's hand in his, and then knelt down in front of her, "Kara my wife, my love, my best friend, I sincerely thank you from the bottom of my heart for loving me, being a part of my life, accepting me for who I am, being supportive during hard times, putting up with all the bullshit from the past two years, and," Mark paused for a moment, and said as his eyes slightly swelled up with tears, "Thank you for giving me the child I've always wanted and dreamed of. I love you. In fact, I love you even more now than I did when we first met."

Mark as Kara's eyes also slightly swelled up with tears, leaned in and kissed her on the lips.

The kiss quickly turned into a very deep and passionate kiss…

It lasted for quite some time…

They then broke away from the kiss, and looked deeply into each others eyes. So deep it was if though they could see one another's souls.

Mark stood up.

Kara stood up as well and said while she put her arms around Mark and began to passionately kiss him again, "Oh Mark, I love you so much, and I thank you too. Thank you for being you and being in my life."

Mark put both his hands on Kara's soft behind and lifted her off her feet while she wrapped her legs around his waist.

They continued to passionately kiss…

Mark swung Kara's body around, quickly put his arms under her legs, carried her into the cottage and closed the door behind them. Then into the bedroom, where they entwined together like two naked souls put into the beautiful body of one, and made slow, careful love by candle light until the early morning sun came up.

Afterwards, the two of them fell into a deep magical sleep, and didn't awake until late afternoon…

For the both of them it was all so heavenly…

As all things in our Earthly life should be…

13

One month after Mark and Kara's vacation it was mid-October, the weather was mildly warm during the day, it was cool at night, the trees leaves had all changed to their beautiful rustic fall colors, and things just kept getting better and better for Mark and Kara. Mark did a few more big book promotions, he did a couple of interviews on local and national radio shows, he won two more writer's awards, and sales of his books were skyrocketing. Things were really going well, so well that the both of them were living on such an emotional high that it seemed as though nothing could bring them down, and nothing did. They were so happy and grateful for the wonderful things that had been happening, that they totally forgot about all the recent bad that had taken place. They had finally gotten to move forward, which felt great. For Mark especially, it felt like the mysterious cosmic physics of the metaphysical universe had finally turned around and started to work in his favor. He felt anything was possible, and nothing within reason was out of his reach; not even the sky. All things were good; good including the new book he was working on; that was going very well also. The writing process was moving along a lot faster than normal for Mark, which was a good thing because his publisher fronted him quite a substantial amount of money for the finished manuscript. They also gave him a deadline, which Mark didn't care about because he knew that if he kept up at the pace he'd been working that he would be done way before the deadline. He was also pretty confident the company wouldn't turn it away either, so day-by-day, week-by-week, hour-by-hour, Mark kept crunching away at it. Eight hours a day, forty hours a week is what he dedicated to the manuscript. Just like a regular everyday job, Mark stuck to it and made sure he worked every single scheduled day. Five days on with weekends off; he even worked some Saturdays. Not usually though, just sometimes. Other times they were spent doing things with Kara, or they were spent doing small public appearances, or they were spent just simply relaxing. If Mark or the both of them had to leave town for his work, Mark then took the manuscript with him and designated time to work on it. He really dedicated himself to it, and Kara as usual, unconditionally loved him, and fully supported everything.

They also were very seldom ever apart, they did and went almost everywhere together, and they didn't mind that at all. They loved it, and they loved each other very much. To them it was usually a bummer if they couldn't be together.

Sometimes though, Mark did have to go away on book business and Kara had to stay home for something. It was usually something that had to do with an appointment she had to keep, and to them that was generally an inconvenience. But it was never usually for very long, so it gave them something else to look forward to when Mark got home. Plus, business was business; personal time would just have to wait. Especially when it came to the baby girl Kara was carrying inside her, if she had an obstetrician appointment that coincided with something Mark absolutely had to do, then she couldn't go, and one time she didn't. Once, Kara had an appointment on the same day Mark had a big out-of-state-event that he had to attend to; it was in St Louis, Missouri. So one day prior, Mark flew to St Louis while Kara stayed home. His book rep Andrea went with him, which was okay, but Mark would have rather had Kara with him. But such is life; one can't have everything, so Mark made the best of it all and tried to have a good time.

Which he did.

He spent the day of the event as usual, signing books, smiling, talking with people from all different walks of life, and shaking a lot of hands. And just like the more recent book conventions Mark attended, all of his books completely sold out, plus it was a lot of fun.

Times were good, and Mark was feeling good.

It was just too bad that Kara couldn't have been with him, because she would have really enjoyed herself, as she always did.

Of course though, she also enjoyed anything that had to do with the baby. So going to her appointment wasn't so bad for her, and for Mark as well; it was kind of exciting.

It was especially exciting for Mark, as it always was, and he couldn't wait for the convention to be over with, and when it finally was, Mark couldn't wait to hear how things went with Kara's appointment. So he rushed back to the hotel where he was staying, and because he forgot to take his phone with him, he hurried to his room.

When he got there he quickly let himself in.

He searched for his phone.

At first he couldn't find it, but after searching for a moment, Mark found it and immediately called Kara.

He got no answer, so he called again.

Her phone kept going to voice-mail, so Mark stopped for a moment and paced around the room.

He stopped pacing and tried again.

Then after a few rings, Kara finally answered, "Hello."

"Hey it's me. How you doing?"

"Good. Yourself?"

"Great!"

"Good. How was the convention?"

"Good, everything went well. Met a lot of people, and again, all of my books sold out."

"Wow! That's great Mark!"

"Yeah. Um, so, how did your appointment go?"

"Good, everything's going the way things are supposed to go. So far I'm healthy, and the baby, well she's healthy and developing at a normal pace."

"Wow, that's great! Did you get more pictures?"

"Yep. I sure did."

"Cool, I can't wait to see them. Of course I can't wait to see you either, I. Oh, speaking of seeing you, are you gonna be able to pick me up from the airport, or do you still have to take your sister to the doctor?"

"Her car won't be done for another two days, so yeah, I still have to take her. Sorry."

"Naw, don't be sorry. I'll just take a cab then."

"Are you sure? Because your mother said she would come and get you."

"Yeah, I'm positive."

"Okay then. You wanna call your mother and let her know, or would you like me to?"

"No, it's been a while since I've spoken to her. So I'd better call her, don't want her to think I've forgotten about her. If you know what I mean?"

"Oh yeah, I sure do. So, I'll see you some time tomorrow?"

"Yep, you sure will."

"Okay sounds good. Do me a favor though."

"What's that?"

"Call me when you're on your way to the airport, and then call me when you get in."

"Okay, we'll do. Love you, and I'll see you."

"K, love you too, and have a safe trip."

"I'll try, and love you bye."

"Bye."

Mark pressed his phone's hang up button, tossed it to the bed, and went into the bathroom to shower.

14

The next day, Mark's flight got in around three pm, and he got home shortly after four. Doing as Kara had asked, Mark called her while he was on his way to the airport earlier that day in St Louis. But when he got home, unlike how she had asked him to, Mark wanted to surprise her, so he decided not to call her. He instead, after he let himself in, hurried and unpacked, put all of his travel things away, and then patiently strolled around the house while he waited for her to get home.

The doorbell rang…

It rang again…

Wondering who it could be, Mark went quickly to the door and looked out a side window.

Seeing that it was a State Police Officer, Mark quickly grabbed the door by its handle and swiftly swung it open.

He sternly asked as he stared the man in the eye, "Yeah, can I help you?"

"Are you Mark Morgan?"

"Yes I am."

"Is your wife a Mrs. Kara Taylor Morgan?"

"Yes."

"And do the both of you own a white two thousand and twelve Dodge Challenger SRT?"

"Yes we do. Now what's this all about?"

"Well Sir, my name is Douglas Bradley. I work for the Michigan State Police, and I'm one of the chief automobile accident inspectors for this county." Mark's heart began to sink, "I'm sorry to inform you that your wife's car, with her in it, was found turned over in a ditch not to far from here, only about thirty minutes ago," Mark went numb. "I'm also sorry to inform you that she was pronounced dead at the scene."

"You're kidding me?"

"No Sir, I' am not, I would never do that…"

Mark just stood for a moment…

He didn't know what to say…

The officer continued, "Now I know this is hard, but I need you to come to the hospital with me so her body can be fully identified, and so we can finish our report. Can you do that for me?"

Standing in complete numbing shock, and also feeling sick to his stomach, Mark barley managed to get the words, "Yeah, sure," out of his mouth.

His whole body felt as though it was quickly being poisoned…

The officer said, "Okay then, if you will follow me."

"Sure." Mark replied…

Stepping out of the house, Mark closed the door behind him, and followed the officer to his cruiser.

He just couldn't believe what he had just heard, and he was shaking from the inside-out with sickening nervousness.

Why is this happening? Is all he could think. It was as if he was dreaming and nothing around him seemed real.

At the hospital after he identified Kara, Mark stood next to her in a morgue room, and blankly stared at her lifeless body. She was so beautiful to him, her Auburn hair so long and pretty, her skin so perfect and soft. She looked just like a sleeping angel, and he didn't understand why this had happened. Mark desperately tried to wrap his mind around the whole thing, but he couldn't. What did they do to deserve this? He didn't know, and he was so confused that his whole body was numb.

Why? Mark thought, What did we do? Why, why, why? Why is this happening? Everything was all going so good. We were supposed to…

Mark began to cry, and he leaned to Kara and cried harder as he hugged her; he didn't want to let her go, she was everything to him, and he couldn't let go, and he wouldn't let go. He just kept crying and crying, and saying, "Come on baby, wake up so we can go home. Come on, we've got a lot to talk about. Come on baby. Come on." If he could have, Mark would have poured every ounce of energy from his body, heart, and soul into her just to bring her and the child she held within her womb back, but he couldn't, and it just wasn't fair.

Mark's tears turned to hysteria, and he just kept hugging and squeezing Kara while he cried.

His mother eventually walked in behind him, touched his shoulder, tried to calm him, and said, "Come on Mark. Come on, she wouldn't want this from you."

Mark tearfully replied, "No, No, Not until they both wake up."

He gently rubbed Kara's swollen womb, and he wouldn't let go…

"Shh, come on Mark. Lets go someplace and calm down."

He still wouldn't let go. He kept rubbing Kara, hugging her, and crying; he was a mess.

"Come on Mark." His mother said again.

"No, they're both gonna wake up, and then we'll go home.

We've got a lot to do."

"Mark, you're not doing either one of you any good. Now come on."

With his Mother's words, Mark slowly turned from Kara, tearfully looked into his mother's eyes, and said, "It's just not fair, it's not fair."

"I know honey, I know." She replied as she tried to comfort him, "I know." She hugged him tightly and said while he cried on her shoulder, "Shh, I know it's not fair baby, I know, now try and calm down so we can take a long walk and have a long talk. Can you do that right now for me; please?"

"Yeah, I think so..."

"Okay, now come on."

Mark's mother then slowly walked him out of the room, and they went for a long walk. Eventually she calmed him down, and that helped him put his head together; but now he would probably never be the same again.

15

Four days after Mark got the untimely shocking news about Kara, her sad, sad funeral service took place, and even though Mark had it announced that the service was private, because of his local celebrity status, all sorts of people from all sorts of different places showed up anyways and gave their condolences. Mark was very thankful for this, but also at the same time, he was very, very annoyed about it. Yeah, he understood that people were only trying to give him and all the family involved their support, but, what part about, "Private," didn't anyone understand? Most of them never even knew Kara, and if it wasn't for Mark being who he was, none of them would have been there in the first place. But, oh well, Mark thought as he dealt with it the best he could, being annoyed and *acting like a dick won't bring my wife and child back. So I'd better fake my way through the day the best I can… Act strong, and don't show any sign of weakness. Be tough, be tough for Kara and the baby. Don't let anyone know how upset you really are. In fact, don't be upset. Just get through this fucking goddamn forsaken day… Try to keep moving forward, and definitely don't let anyone here know what you're thinking… Especially the people that showed up only because their fans of your books, definitely don't let them know. Just shake hands, smile, and say thanks for coming… That's all you have to do. And don't talk about books, if anyone tries to, just give them a quick brush off, because today is definitely not the day for it. Of course now, I'm not sure if any day is ever again gonna be a good time to… Man what am I gonna do? Just get through the day, that's all I have to do… For* now…

And that's all Mark did, just like a Tough Marine doing his or her sworn duty, Mark went through the service, the wake, the procession, and the burial with hardly any show of emotion. He shook hands, he hugged people, he said all sorts of different things, he even smiled a few times. But it wasn't genuine, in fact for Mark, nothing that day was, and he didn't know if anything ever would be again. He felt just totally numb; numb all over his body, and numb about everything. Nothing was real, and nothing felt real. It was like to him that he was living in a daydream, a rather sad and ugly daydream.

Part of Mark didn't even know if he was alive anymore, he felt so dead that he really couldn't tell if he was coming or going. And at the very end of the day, after Kara's casket was lowered into the ground, and everyone had left, a cool breeze blew across the grass, the sun began to go down, and Mark just mindlessly sat alone, and blankly stared into the distance. Focusing on nothing, or not even really seeing anything in his sights, Mark sat catatonic, and just mindlessly stared until the sun was gone, and the nighttime fully fell in around him.

He was truly alone…

16

Two days after Kara's funeral Mark still felt numb and mindless. He hadn't really eaten much, he didn't really speak to anyone besides his mother, and after he got home, he didn't really go anywhere either. He didn't work, he didn't accept phone calls from work, and he really didn't even want to think about work. He didn't sleep much either. He just laid out in a recliner in front of a television with a remote in his hand and smoked cigarette after cigarette, which was something he never usually did. At one time though, for a short period, when Mark was younger he smoked. But he got sick of it really quick so he gave it up. But for some reason, probably because of recent events, something triggered in his mind and he started again.

He also started to drink, which is something he had always done in moderation, and had always done cleanly and responsibly. But not now; now he was filthy, and very sloppy with it, and he didn't really care. There were empty and half-full beer cans strewn about the whole house, there was overflowing ashtrays on almost every living room end table, and empty fast food containers were just carelessly tossed about on the floors.

The room that Mark and Kara had prepared for the baby was also completely wrecked. The night he had got home from Kara's funeral, in one fit of blind rage he destroyed it and everything in it. He wiped out everything from the brand new crib and furniture that he and Kara bought together. To even punching holes in the walls with his bare hands, and ripping all the brand-new baby clothes to shreds. He kicked all the widows out of the room and ripped the lighting fixtures from the ceiling; he was mad beyond belief. He had managed to hold his emotions together the whole day, but for obvious reasons when he got home and saw that room, all of his held up emotions just totally let loose.

He had even injured his hands in the process, and his palms were cut pretty deeply. Mark needed stitches, and he knew he needed them. But he didn't care; he just bandaged his hands really tight and went about doing what it was he was going to do, because he just didn't care. He wasn't going to go to the doctor. In fact, the only place he was going to go to was the local liquor store, and the occasional food take out place that was just around the corner from his house. Other than that, Mark wasn't going anywhere, or doing anything. Not even showering or shaving, which was something he was really starting to need. For only four days of no grooming, he was starting to look real scruffy, and he also began to reek with the foul stench of B.O., stale cigarettes, and skunked beer. He was really starting to become a mess, and ten days later he was. His beard was filthy, his clothes were filthy, his hair was dirty, the house was a complete wreck, and Mark had been drinking so much that he couldn't tell whether he was coming or going. He didn't even really know what time of day it was, what day it was, or what month it was. He was in bad shape; he even pissed himself a few times without notice, and just laid in it.

He was almost as low as one could possibly go, he felt no hope, he wanted to die, and he couldn't stand it. But he also couldn't figure out how to escape the nightmare he was in.

Why? At times he desperately wanted to. But he just couldn't. Sometimes when he would pass out in his chair, Mark would cry out Kara's name in his sleep, and then abruptly wake up in a trembling alcoholic sweat. Other times he would just cry for hours, and then pass out.

He needed help, but he didn't know how to get it. He just couldn't get out.

He was confused...

He desperately wanted out, but he couldn't get out. He didn't know how. "Why?" he cried...

The confusion just wouldn't let him go, the alcohol had totally taken over his mind, and he began to slowly go insane from it. At times he even had horrible hallucinations of hellish-looking creatures with wings coming after him and trying to rip his body to pieces. He would try to run from them, but he never got away, they would always catch him and viciously rip his flesh from his bones while he screamed out in agony. Of course it was all in his mind, but he couldn't tell the difference.

He had also heard voices, all sorts of different voices, voices that said vicious and very violent things to him, "Kill yourself. Bastard! Fuck you! Fuck your Mother! Fuck your Daughter! You killed the bitch! Fuck yourself! I own your soul. We have your baby!"

It was all so frightening. He was living in a true nightmare, a nightmare that he kept trying to wake from, but just couldn't.

Then one day by some miracle, Mark managed to see himself in a mirror, and it was then he had a wakeup call; woke up, saw truth in his reflection, and it made him sick, and it was then he knew what he had to do. He needed another new beginning, and he was going to go and find it. But first he would clean himself up, throw out the cigarettes and the booze. He would then call a maid service to clean up the house, and call his mother to let her know that he was alright. He would leave a message on his voice mail and let people know where and how he was. He would then head up to the Thunder Bay cottage, and try to find peace there, because he had finally had enough.

No more will I suffer, no more will I cry, and no more will I harm myself.

17

Four days after Mark awoke from his fourteen-day drunken breakdown, he left a message on his voice mail that said, "Hi, you've reached Mark. I can't come to the phone right now because I'm on my way to the cottage. I'll be back in two weeks. Don't bother showing up there or calling my car phone because I won't answer. I need time to myself. Thank you, and I promise I'll return your call when I get back." He then shut his phone off, and tossed it onto a table as he made his way out of the house and to his car.

Hopping into the car, Mark started the engine, backed out of the driveway, and quickly took off down the road.

Three hours and twenty minutes later he arrived at the cottage and pulled into its short gravel driveway. Putting the car in park, Mark shut the engine off and sat for a moment. He stared at the dreary wintry scene of the peaceful-looking cottage. It was slightly covered with a light dusting of freshly fallen snow, and to Mark it was majestically beautiful looking. It gave him an inner feeling of peace. He remembered what a wonderful time he and Kara had the last time they were there, and that made him feel warm on the inside. It all seemed so tranquil that he wished he could live in the moment forever, and for a short brief one he did; he felt good again.

Taking a deep breath, Mark hit the car's, "Trunk open," button and got out.

Shutting the car's door behind him and stepping to the trunk, Mark reached in and grabbed the few bags of groceries that he had stopped and bought at a local store in the small town of Ossineke as he passed through.

He slammed the trunk shut and made his way to the cottage's front door.

He unlocked it and let himself inside.

Closing the door behind him as he stepped into a formal mudroom, Mark then, in order to shake the snow from his wet shoes, quickly kicked his feet against a brown doorway rug that sat on a white and black, hard ceramic tiled floor. After, He made his way to the cottage's small kitchen and set the bags of groceries down onto a counter, flipped on a light switch, and stood still for a moment. It was quiet there, as it always was, and Mark stood and listened to the silence. It was peaceful; the kind of peace Mark had wanted and needed. There was almost literally no sound, and it had a real calming affect on him, which was something he had so desperately wanted, and it was also one of the reasons he had always went there. He loved the peaceful energy the cottage and its surroundings gave off. When he was there it always felt like he was on a different planet, and the rest of the world didn't exist. For Mark, it was true serenity; maybe being there would help to heal his wounds; wounds that, in order for him to live again, needed to close. Close and become simple scars, the kind of scars that we all carry, but the kind that don't prevent us from living. Because deep down inside, Mark really wanted to live again. Yes he missed Kara, and he didn't understand why what had happened with her happened, and he also had some flashbacks about the things that had went on with his uncle, and was somewhat still sad about. But Mark, under no circumstances, wanted to keep reliving it all, ever. So, after he put the groceries away, he went through the cottage and prepared it to stay in. He turned up the furnace, flipped on the water heater, turned the well pump on, and got the air out of all the plumbing. He then started a small fire in the cottage's cozy little living room fireplace. Afterwards, he sat down in a comfortable reclining chair with an attached footstool and wrote out a plan and schedule to follow. He figured that by making the plan and strict schedule, if he forced himself to stick to it, that it would help him to move completely forward and only reflect on the past, not live in it. Plus, writing was one of those few things that Mark found comfort in when he sat down and made himself do it. It helped him to forget, and when things got bad, or seemed to get bad, writing always had a way of taking him out of the darkness.

So that's what he did. Mark wrote and made his game plan, and one of his plans was to get rid of the other house and everything in it. He would make the Thunder Bay cottage his permanent residence, and since he now had more money then he would ever be able to spend, he would, except for a few personal things, give it all away. But, he wouldn't just simply give things to anyone, he would make sure it was all donated to the right people, especially the house. Mark wouldn't just give that away; he would check into various organizations first. Then he would decide, *Heck,* Mark thought while he wrote his plans, *I might just donate the house with everything in it. Yeah, that just might make things a whole lot easier... Hmm? I don't know, we'll see though? There's a lot to do...*

Mark sat and blankly stared for a moment...

He gazed into the dancing fire that was peacefully crackling away in the fireplace, and then got up and turned on a small radio. Turning its tuner through some static and skipping past a few stations, Mark found some soft music, and went back to writing his plans. He became so engrossed in them that he didn't even notice that outside it had begun to snow, and it wasn't a light snow either, it had begun to snow really hard.

Mark also didn't hear it when a local weather advisory came over the radio saying that, "All of North Eastern Michigan was now under a severe snow storm warning. One to two feet, along with blowing and gusting snow is to be expected for overnight."

He just kept writing, writing as hours passed, and for so long that nighttime fell, the fire in the fireplace died down, the snow outside piled and piled, and he became so relaxed, that he eventually nodded off and fell asleep right where he sat.

18

Waking up early the next morning, Mark opened his eyes, wearily looked around the cozy little living room of the cottage with blurry morning vision, and closed them back shut. He let out a loud roaring yawn while he stretched out his arms and legs.

Opening his eyes again, he looked around the room for a moment with better focus.

He stood up and stretched again, went and took a look through the curtains of a sliding glass door that was at the back side of the of the living room, which also led the way to the screened-in porch that faced the beach and bay, and said, "Holy Shit! look at all of that snow! Fuck! It really must have come down last night. Hmm, and I missed it."

He turned from looking out at the snow, to turning his ears to the radio as he then made his way to the cottage's tiny bathroom to do his morning duty. He listened to part of the local news that talked about last night's storm, and how it had shut down most of Michigan's Northeastern counties. Which were, Alpena, Alcona, parts of Iosco, Oscoda, and Montmorency, and how it had been one of the worst storms that part of Michigan had seen in a long time. Things including roads, schools, government, and businesses were going to be shut down for a few days.

Cool! Mark thought with excitement as he finished up in the bathroom and made his way into the kitchen, *I know what I'm gonna do today, I'm going snowmobiling. Must eat first though.*

Shuffling through the cupboards, then the refrigerator, Mark, after he got everything he needed together in order to cook, began to prepare himself a big breakfast. The kind of breakfast that was going to keep him full for most of the day because Mark planned on staying gone until sundown. *Heck,* Mark thought while he cooked, *I might even stay out past sundown. We'll see though, I'm just gonna ride until I can't ride anymore, or the snowmobile breaks down... Yeah, let's hope that doesn't happen. Just in case though, remember to pack the small shortwave walkie-talkie, and try not to stray too far... Shit! I hope there's gas in one of the shed cans. If not, I think I might be screwed. Man I hope not, because I really wanna go...*

Continuing to cook while he tuned his ears back to the radio, Mark hummed along with the music and thought, Did I hook a trickle charger to that things battery? Hmm? Yeah, I'm pretty sure the last time I was here I did it before I left... I know I did the jet-ski's and four-wheeler's... Not to sure about the snowmobile's though. Oh well, I guess when I'm done here I'll find out. Ha, this will be the first time that thing has ever even been used. Hmm, it's been so long since I've even driven one, I might have forgotten how to. Naw, I'm sure it'll all come back to me.

Mark kept cooking, thinking, and preparing his breakfast, which ended up being so big that it filled two regular-size plates, and one small one. He really wanted to fill up, and after he was done cooking, he set up at a small table in the living room, opened the adjacent sliding glass door curtains that gave a beautiful picture window view of the beach and bay, and sat down and ate.

19

Shortly after Mark finished eating, and he let his food settle, he rinsed off his dishes and silverware in the kitchen sink, and left them in it. He went to the cottage's small bedroom, that also had windows facing the beach and bay. He went to the room to change his clothes, but when he stepped into it and saw Kara's favorite silky, purple, summer gown, neatly draped over the back of a wooden vanity chair, he hesitated. It was the same gown she wore every night to bed the last time they were there, and she had also put it on every time they made love. Mark had just somehow forgotten about it, and he stood frozen in spot, and just stared at it.

His insides began to tremble…

The sight of the gown triggered Kara's presence, everything they had done the last time they were there flooded into Mark's mind, and filled the room with her energy.

He started to feel sick…

He closed his eyes and took a really deep breath, then let it out, and whispered to himself while he kept his eyes closed, "Don't do this Mark, don't feel this way… You know it's time to move on." He took another deep breath, and let it out while he opened his eyes and said, "Okay, you can do this." He stepped to the chair and picked up the pretty gown.

It still lightly had Kara's earthly feminine smell embedded into its silky fibers, and Mark's senses picked it up.

He trembled again, and wished that he could once more feel her soft warm touch…

The smell of her on the gown triggered Kara's presence even more in Mark's mind, and he immediately had flashing visions of her, and how things were shortly before she died. He had loved her so much, he wished like hell that she could be there. He wanted it so badly that holding the gown was almost like holding her. He didn't want to put it down, but he knew he had to. He knew if he was to move forward, that he had to let go of even the smallest of things. Not the gown though; not yet. He decided after he took a deep breath and exhaled it, that the gown would be one of the things that he would hang onto for a while. Almost all of the rest of her other things would have to go though. So, after he mindfully forced himself to stop trembling from the inside-out, he sat down onto the bedroom's soft double bed, carefully folded up the gown, tucked it into a nightstand drawer, stood up, took another deep breath, and got himself ready for a long day of snowmobiling.

20

The day of snowmobiling for Mark was everything that he had hoped it to be, absolutely nothing went wrong. To him, it was almost a picture-perfect day. The freshly fallen snow was just right; it wasn't to packed or powdery, the air wasn't to cold, and it wasn't to warm. There was no wind, and it was quiet. Plus for most of the day it was overcast and hazy, which gave everything around the area a real serene, peaceful look. It was beautiful, and Mark loved it. It all made him feel so good, and to him it was as if time had stood still. Nothing from his past mattered, only the here and now. He was feeling true bliss, and after he got himself ready, he put on a snow suit and went outside. He was immediately greeted by the deep, beautiful, white snow that had fallen overnight. It was truly an amazing site. It was also amazing to Mark how the clean, fresh, white blanket of snow made everything look, and how quiet it was. There was no sound; the deep snow muffled it, and all Mark could hear was the distant ringing coming from his inner ears, and the faint, far-off hum of a Great Lakes ice breaker's ship's engine that was making its way through the bay. It was all so truly beautiful, so truly beautiful that one could say it was definitely Mother Nature at one of her very finest moments.

After Mark got lucky and found a full five-gallon plastic can of gas in one of the cottage's utility sheds, he made his way with can-in-hand through the deep snow to another shed, and opened it's barn-like doors. He went inside, shuffled around for a funnel, found one, and carefully poured the gas into the tank of his snowmobile. He set the plastic gas can to the side, and checked the snowmobile's engine oil, then the coolant level. Seeing that they were both full, he unplugged and unhooked the trickle charger from the snowmobile's battery; that he had obviously remembered to hook up last time he was there. He set that to the side. Then with the turn of a key, and the press of a button, Mark cranked the snowmobile's engine over once; it immediately fired up.

Waiting for the engine to warm up, Mark shuffled around the shed for his full-face helmet and insulated gloves.

He found them and put them on.

Then, by quickly twisting the snowmobile's handlebar grip throttle, and immediately letting go, Mark revved it's powerful, four stroke engine a couple of times.

Glancing at the snowmobile's coolant gauge, and seeing that the engine was warm enough, Mark jumped on the machine, slammed the throttle around, and blasted out of the shed like a bat out of hell. But abruptly stopped in the yard, jumped off the snowmobile, and jogged back to the shed through the deep snow; he had suddenly realized that he forgot to shut the doors, and he decided that it would be a good idea to go back and shut them, so he did.

After he was done, Mark jogged back to the still-running snowmobile, hopped on it and took off.

In order to get a good feel for the powerful machine, Mark did some laps around the perimeter of the his property. After he was confident he had the feel for it, he took off down the desolate, snow-filled road, and headed for the small town of Ossineke. If he was going to ride for a while, he needed to get to a gas station and completely fill the snowmobile's tank. The gas from the five gallon can wasn't quite going to be enough. He just hoped that one of the stations in town would be open, because man there was a lot of snow. More than likely one of them would be though, and one was. So when Mark got into town, he stopped at one and topped off the snowmobile's gas tank.

Then after he went inside and grabbed some bottled waters, he paid the station clerk, left, and took off for the trails. He went everywhere he could possibly think of, and because he did, he found himself having to stop for gas and water a few more times that day, which was okay with him, because everywhere he went was so marvelous and beautiful looking, that Mark felt like he could ride forever, and he had no real plans of when he was going to stop. For him, it was all so heavenly, that if he'd had it his way, he would have never gone back. With every trail he traveled, with every road he rode upon, with every lakeside path that took him along the shores of the cold-looking waters of Lake Huron and Thunder Bay, Mark felt absolutely farther and farther away from his past. It all felt so wonderful to him, and it was all so breathtaking that it was like being in a white wintry dream, and time was standing still. In fact, for Mark it almost was; he had no sense of it, nor did he keep track of it, and nor did he care. He just kept riding on and on, and seeing every sight that he could possibly see.

At one point of his ride, Mark even made his way into parts of downtown Alpena, which, for him was really cool because he always loved that city. To him, for some mysterious reason, that city was a very warm and welcoming place to be. Plus in all the years he had been going to that part of Michigan, he had never seen the city snow-covered before. So why pass up the chance to see it?

Mark then, after he tooled around the city for awhile and saw everything there was he wanted to see, made his way back towards Ossineke, and also did a quick ride around Partridge Point and Squaw Bay. He figured, *Why not, it's on my way. Plus I've never seen the Partridge Point Lighthouse at this time of year. Probably looks really cool with all this snow on and around it. Man I should have brought a camera with me. Hmm, oh well, maybe next time. If there is one? There's no telling when it'll snow like this again. Hmm, who knows, it could be tomorrow? More than likely not though.*

Mark kept riding…

He kept riding, and rode around Partridge Point until he stopped for a moment to look at the Lighthouse. It was an awesome sight to Mark. He marveled at its authentic architectural beauty, wished again that he had brought a camera with him because it just looked so beautiful covered in snow, and took off riding again.

Traveling down some more trails after he went around Partridge Point, Mark saw some deer, a pretty good-sized black bear, and wished again that he would have brought a camera with him, *Damn it!* He thought. *That bear was amazing-looking, of course though if I would have brought a camera, I probably wouldn't have seen it, or the fucking thing would have mauled me to death if I did.*

Mark then emerged from the trail and road around the full perimeter of Squaw Bay, and made his way to the beach shore of the lake. He planned on following it all the way back to the cottage, and beyond. And he did, until he was stopped by the mouth of the Devil's river. When Mark got there he stopped and thought, *Shit! I forgot about this obstacle. Man, it's too bad it's not frozen. If it was, I could just drive across… Hmm? What to do?*

Ah, that's a good idea, and hell, you only live once, and besides, its not really that wide. Plus with enough speed I should be able to make it.

Mark turned the snowmobile around and headed in the opposite direction of the river mouth. His plan was to race towards it as fast as he could, and hopefully hydroplane across it, and after he stopped and turned the snowmobile back around, that's exactly what he did. He slammed the throttle around as hard as he could and raced really fast towards the river mouth. Then, right as he got to the edge of the water, he stood hunched up full of adrenaline and jerked back on the snowmobile's steering handles as hard as he could, and with a high-flying rooster tail of freezing cold water trailing behind and around him, Mark and the snowmobile swiftly hydroplaned, and blasted across the water top like a speeding jet boat, and safely made it to the other side.

Soaking wet and still full of adrenaline, Mark didn't even bother to stop or look back, he just sat back down and kept racing along the shore.

He did slow down when he went by the cottage though. But after he took a quick glance at it, he sped back up again, and raced all the way to the opening point of the shore where Thunder Bay opened up into open water. He slowed down when he got there, and slowly drove all the way out to the very edge of the point and stopped.

He looked out across the bay…

He looked out across the open waters of Lake Huron, and he could see small Scarecrow Island in the distance. He could also see a freighter way out in the water entering the bay through the Nine Mile Can. It made him feel calm and at peace, and he kept gazing out across the open waters. It was like he was staring into a mystical magical abyss that went on to the edge of the universe, and beyond. *What's out there? Where does it all go? Does it even end? And what is the invisible exhilarating energy coming from this place, this place of absolute wonder? And why am I lured to it? I can feel it, I wish I could become one with it. The water speaks to me, the waves gently roll, the air is so fresh. It's all so magical. So, so magical,* Mark thought and kept thinking while he gazed at the beautiful scene. *Why can't I ever get enough of this place? Someday I'm never gonna leave. I want to die here and just float away into eternity.*

Mark kept thinking, and as it always was, the energy there where he was, was just so electrifying to him that he didn't want to leave. It was a very spiritual, metaphysical experience, and if one was still, silent, and also free of mind, no matter what season it was you could always hear a song coming from the trees of the nearby forest. It was as if the tress themselves were creating the music, and Mark stood and listened to it; as he always did each and every time he was there. It was all so soothing, and very, very peaceful. Sometimes he wished he could be wrapped up and become one with the energy that surrounded the place, and then blissfully float around in it forever. Why he had always felt this way, he had no clue, he just did, and at times it consumed his whole being. He also knew he couldn't stay forever, he got really wet when he crossed the river, and he was starting to get cold from it. But before he would go, Mark would keep the snowmobile's engine running, which would help a little in keeping him warm, and he would stay and watch the now fully-emerged sun; the sun that was held captive all day long by the hazy gray clouds that covered and blocked out most of its bright warm light, go down.

As he watched, Mark tingled with Goosebumps, and he became frozen in time while the fiery orange sun slowly dropped below the horizon and lit the sky and far off waters with an array of warm beautiful hues. Warm beautiful hues that slowly changed from brilliant purples, greens, oranges, reds, and gold as it dropped.

He thought of Kara for a moment...

He envisioned her soft, warm smiling face, and he could feel her presence. It was as if she was there with him, but he couldn't touch her or see her. All he could do is visualize and try to feel her.

But it wasn't real, and Mark knew it wasn't. But it was oh so wonderful. So wonderful that under his full-faced mask and helmet, Mark had shed a few tears of joy. He was happy for the time they'd had together. It was an honor, and no matter how much it hurt, Mark wasn't going to let her loss bring him down anymore. He was going to be happy and grateful for the fact that he had gotten to share part of his life with her, and how it was a true blessing to have known such a wonderful person. Even though he had wished so badly that she could be there, especially during this picture perfect moment, from here on out, Mark decided he wasn't going to grieve anymore. Everyday was going to be a new and exciting day.

With those thoughts flowing through his mind, Mark kept watching, and the sun went fully down, nighttime came, the stars filled the blackened sky, and Mark decided it was time to head back to the cottage. He was now extremely tired; so tired that when he got back he left the snowmobile out, went into the cottage from the beach side screen porch door, got out of all his wet clothes, put on something comfortable to sleep in, grabbed a blanket, got a drink, used the bathroom, cuddled up in his recliner with the blanket draped over him, and quickly fell asleep.

He slept all the way until the next morning, and woke up extremely sore from all the riding he had done. In fact he was so sore that, that day he didn't really do much of anything besides, shower, eat, write, and watch DVDS and videotapes on a small portable television. Mark's body just hurt to bad to do much of anything else, so his other plans would just have to wait a day or so.

Didn't matter anyways, he had eleven days....

21

The day after Mark spent lounging around from soreness, was a pretty nice day for it being wintertime in northern Michigan. The sun was out, there wasn't a cloud in the sky, the wind was barely blowing, and the counties were all up and running again. Mark had woken up late, because he was up late, and he was still somewhat sore. But unlike the day before, he was a functioning sore. The day before there was no way he was going to do much of anything, he just couldn't. But today he could. So, he got up, stretched, and then started his day with a good breakfast. He after breakfast and a shower, with the help from a snow-blower, a broom and a shovel, cleared snow from his car, and various places around the cottage. Places such as the small driveway, the front and back walkways, around both front and back porches, all the sheds, the path that led from the driveway to the front door, and the perimeter of the cottage. After he was done and he put away all the tools of the snow-clearing trade, Mark went to the beach side of the cottage and fired up the snowmobile. He was surprised it started right up after sitting out for a day and a half.

After he let it's engine warm up for a moment, Mark drove the snowmobile back to the shed and put it away. He planned on going riding again, probably later on in the week though, he was still a little sore, and he had other things to do, so riding would have to wait.

One of the things he had to do was to stick with his plan. While he was clearing the snow, Mark made a mental plan to pack up all of the clothes that Kara kept at the cottage, and donate them probably to a used clothing store or something. Except the purple gown; he decide he would keep that. But before he could do any of it, Mark would have to get some boxes or something. So, after he went in and changed from his snow removal clothes to some regular street clothes, Mark locked up the cottage, hopped in the car, and took a drive into Alpena, which was a safe thing to do since he had heard over the radio that all of the main roads were cleared, and the county, along with all the others were up and running again.

After Mark got there, he drove around for a while site seeing. He had done it numerous times before, and he didn't care, because for Mark, site seeing around Alpena and northeastern Michigan never got old. It was always new and refreshing to him, and he would probably do it plenty more times in his life before he died. To him it was one of the few places he had ever been that truly felt like home, and every time he was there, he never wanted to leave. He had business to take care of though, so he didn't drive around for to long, just long enough to see a few things.

When he was done, Mark stopped at a store that specialized in packing and moving supplies and bought a couple of bundles of unmade boxes and strapping tape. He then ventured back to the cottage, arrived, got his supplies out of the car, and went inside.

He made up a couple of boxes and took them into the bedroom. Once he was done packing up all of Kara's clothes, he would then turn around and head back to the city with them, and donate them to the secondhand hand store that he had found while he was driving around. Except the purple nightgown, Mark planned on keeping that. Why? He didn't know. He just did.

He got started…

First he went into Kara's side of the bedroom closet, pulled all of her clothes from their hangers, and neatly laid them out onto the bed.

He carefully folded each piece up, placed it all in one of the boxes, and taped it shut.

Mark then went through her personal vanity dresser, pulled everything out, laid it all onto the bed, and began going through it all.

Not everything that was in the dresser was clothing. There was makeup, there was hair styling stuff, there was undergarments, jewelry, perfumes, lotions, etc.

Mark wondered if the secondhand store would take those things as well. *Probably not,* Mark thought. So for the time being he just concentrated on the clothing; he would figure out later what to do with the other things. For now he would just put those things in a separate box.

I could give it all to Kara's mother, Mark thought, she'd probably appreciate that. Good idea, just remember to label the box, Kara's Mom when you're done..

Mark then abruptly stopped what he was doing and thinking, went out to his car, got a small leather pouch from the trunk, went back inside, and stood in the middle of the living room.

Blankly staring out of the cottage's back window, and gazing at the snow covered beach, and half frozen bay, Mark mindlessly opened the pouch, pulled out a small nine-millimeter pistol, started breathing heavy, and held it to his right temple. He couldn't handle it anymore; the smell of Kara's clothes set him off. Her memory, his loss, their unborn child that died along with her, his uncle, the things that happened with him; everything. All of it. It all just started racing through his head like an out of control freight train, and he could no longer stand it. He was being mentally tortured and all he wanted was silence.

Why did she and the baby have to die? They were the only things that I had truly loved and had left!! Why, why, why! Why did they all die?

Kara's memory flashed before his eyes, his uncle and all the shit that had happened with him flashed before his eyes. His wedding, his unborn child, it all flashed so fast that he couldn't take it. He began to shake. He began to sweat. He pulled the trigger, the gun just clicked, and the sound of the hammer sent him into immediate shock. He instantly froze, broke out in a cold nauseating sweat, then dropped the gun as he violently threw up all over the place, stumbled backwards holding his stomach, pissed himself, fell into a table, fell forward, then collapsed to the floor and passed out.

Everything went silent, and Mark failed…

The gun that he had stopped and bought while originally on his way to the cottage, in his manic breakdown, he forgot to load. Load with the bullets that he had also forgot to purchase. All along, Mark was subconsciously planning on killing himself when he was done with everything. But he failed. He failed because consciously he really wanted to live. Why else would he have forgotten to buy and load the gun with bullets? It seems as though if he had really wanted to do it, he wouldn't have forgotten. Or he was just really stupid? Hmm? Only Mark could answer those questions.

He was in need of some serious help; help that he wasn't going to get from being alone…

22

Forty-eight hours after Mark's suicide attempt, he found himself back in Doctor Susan's office. When he had woken up shaking and drenched in sweat, piss, puke, and on the living room floor of the cottage, he'd had a very real-feeling vision of his uncle. In the vision his uncle lectured him about life and living, and it was the same lecture he had given Mark once before when Mark was young and feeling very troubled.

The vision of his uncle told him, "Mark, no matter how hard things may seem to get, or what someone or something has tried to bind and hold you down with, you never show the world weakness. Cause if you do, that means they've won, and suicide in itself is a sign of weakness, because if you go through with it and succeed, then you've let them win, and don't ever let anyone or anything win over you, or beat you down. Don't even let God or the Devil win; Fuck them both! You don't need them. It's your life, and you deserve to live it, and you better live it. Because if you don't, someone else will live it for you."

Of course when Mark's uncle originally gave him that lecture he was extremely drunk, as he usually was. But Mark, at the time, as he always did, listened to what his uncle had to say, and he took it very seriously. To Mark, especially when he was young, his uncle was a very wise person, he had always looked up to him, and respected him and his words. He had just forgotten about that lecture. If he would have remembered it, Mark probably wouldn't have tried to kill himself, and it wasn't until he had awoken from the vision that he'd had the full realization of what he had almost done. It also had made him realize that he was in need of some serious help. If there was some sort of divine power somewhere in the universe, Mark was thankful for the vision, because he really didn't want to die. Nor did he want to let the spirit of his uncle down, nor Kara's and their unborn child. Mark wanted to truly honor them. So, after he fully got himself together, Mark made a few phone calls with his car's on-board phone system, left everything inside of the cottage the way it was, locked it up, took a cab to the airport, and chartered a small plane to take him back home. Driving would have taken too long, and Mark wanted to get back as soon as possible. Everything else, if he was going to ever fully heal, would just have to wait awhile.

23

Session Six

Stepping into her office and closing the door behind her, Doctor Susan walked to her desk chair, sat down, smiled at Mark, and said, "Well, hello Mr. Morgan. What brings you to see me on this cold and frosty afternoon? Oh wait, let me guess?" Doctor Susan then said with a smile, "You just missed us, and wanted to stop by and say hi?"

Laughing for a second, and abruptly stopping, Mark smiled a half smile at Doctor Susan, and replied, "I wish that was the case." He then paused for a moment and blankly stared.

Doctor Susan immediately sensed something about Mark wasn't quite right. The energy he put off was comparably pretty dark to the last time she had seen him, and even though she knew Kara had just recently died, and for numerous reasons, it was her job to get him to talk about it without her giving any mention to it, or letting on that she knew. So she quickly said, "Well, lay it on me. What's the problem?"

"Well." Mark replied, momentarily paused again, then took a deep breath and let it out, and said, "Hmm, where do I start? Hmm, okay, as you probably already know, because it made local and national news, that my wife, along with our unborn child recently died in a car accident. She had some kind of seizure that was brought on by the pregnancy, and flipped the car into a twelve-foot-ditch."

"Yes I did, and I'm deeply sorry for your loss Mark." Doctor Susan said with a voice of concern.

"Thank you, you have no idea how much that means to me."

"Well you're welcome, and if there's anything you need, I'm here for you. Not just as your doctor either, remember, I'm also your friend."

"Thanks, I'll try to remember that."

"Good. Now how have you been dealing with it?"

"Not well…" Mark replied, and then blankly stared again.

"Would you like to elaborate on that Mark?"

"Yeah I would, and I'm sorry, so much has happened that I just don't know where to begin."

"Well, why don't you begin with what made you come back?"

"Well…" Mark paused and just stared.

"Mark," Doctor Susan said again with a voice of concern, "I can't help you if you don't talk."

Mark quickly snapped out of his blank stare, and blandly said, "I tried to kill myself… I obviously failed though…"

"Really Mark? That's not good. Well the fact that you failed is good, but attempting it, that's not."

"Yeah I know."

"Do you feel like you're going to try again?"

"No, I'm not gonna try again. Nor do I want to."

"Are you sure Mark?"

"Yeah, I'm positive."

"Okay, because if you're not, I'm obligated by law to have you admitted to a psychiatric facility for observation and a full evaluation."

"I'm fully sure."

"Okay, but you have to promise me that once you leave here today, if you even remotely have any thoughts of suicide, that you'll call my counseling hotline."

"Oh trust me, I promise I will."

"Good, now what triggered the attempt? I mean, obviously the loss of your wife and child has been very devastating for you, and again, I'm very, very sorry for your loss. But what were your feelings when you made the attempt?"

"Hmm?" Mark thought for a moment. "Total internal insanity, and an overflow of all sorts of different emotions that all flooded in at once, and kept rapidly changing from one to another. It was unbearable man, and it was like a train wreck just happened in my head."

"Did you do something that you think might have triggered all the mixed racing emotions, or did they just simply start?"

"No, I did something that had more then likely triggered everything."

"Okay, go on."

"Well you see, after I spent, I think about two weeks in the house drinking and smoking myself into total alcohol induced dementia, I somehow one day, miraculously woke out of the haze I had put myself in, and I decided to get my shit together. I then, shortly after, went up north to our cottage. I had a plan. I was gonna be gone by myself for two weeks, you know, get away and have some, "Mark time." I thought, why not? If anything, getting away for awhile should help me feel better, and for a short time it did. Especially when I took a whole day and went snowmobiling, that was great, it really made me feel at peace. The day after was a bitch though, I was so sore from riding the day before that I could hardly move. It sucked, and it was kind of funny and fun at the same time."

"I bet." Doctor Susan said as she leaned back and crossed her legs as usual.

"Yeah, I shouldn't have rode for as long as I did."

"Maybe so, but at least you had fun. Right?"

"Oh yeah, I sure did."

"Well there you go."

"Yeah, lounging around for a day in utter stiffness was kind of fun in itself. I watched a lot of old movies that I hadn't seen in a while. I keep a collection of them at the cottage for those kind of days, or for days that you just simply feel like being lazy."

"Yeah, I have one of those kind of collections myself, of course its all at my home though. My husband and I had always talked about having a small getaway house; somewhere to go to every once in a while. But obviously we never did. Anyway, carry on."

"Well," Mark said as he leaned back and cleared his throat, "the next day when I wasn't feeling as sore, I decided to pack up Kara's things, mainly her clothes, and donate them to a secondhand store. It was part of my written plan."

"Written plan?" Doctor Susan asked with a look of confusion.

Mark replied, "Yeah, the first night there I stayed up really late and wrote out a well-organized what-to-do list. Mainly what to do with Kara's things. I figured if I did that, and stuck to it, and also made it like a regular work schedule, that things for me would be easier, and at first they were. But then…"

"But then?"

"But then it wasn't. When I started packing Kara's clothes up, I just couldn't handle it anymore. They still smelled like her, and when I took notice to it, I just fell apart. It made me crazy, and then like a mindless zombie, I dropped what I was doing, went out to the car, and got the gun I had purchased earlier while on my way up there. I then went back inside, stood in the living room, got the gun out of it's pouch, held it to my head, pulled the trigger. And...

Mark paused and stared again...

Doctor Susan said, "Mark?"

He replied, "Well, lets just say that I immediately passed out. The rest is kind of embarrassing."

"Okay, we'll just go with that then. Carry on"

"I woke up almost twenty hours later to a vision of my uncle lecturing me about something when I was younger. I looked around, realized what I had almost done, and decided I really needed help, and that it was a damn good thing I had forgot to buy the bullets and load that thing. Because if I wouldn't have, I wouldn't be here."

"Yeah really, wow.. Um? Why did you buy the gun in the first place?"

"Well, after I was fully done with taking care of everything, and not everything meaning just Kara's things, I was gonna get rid of all my things as well, including both homes, bank accounts, cars, you name it; everything was gonna go. You know, be responsible and leave no burden behind. Then when I was done, I was just gonna drive off somewhere and do myself in. But part of me really must not have wanted to. I mean why else would I have forgotten the stupid bullets?"

"That maybe true," Doctor Susan said as she uncrossed her legs and sat up straight, "there's usually a reason for everything we do. But do yourself a favor and don't try to figure out why you forgot. Just be thankful you did."

"Oh trust me," Mark replied, "I' am, and I don't wanna die. Especially not like that."

"Good, and we're not gonna let that happen. Now, where's the gun, what did you do with it?"

"It's right where I dropped it, on the living room floor of the cottage."

"Okay good… And how about the written plan you made, where's that?"

"That's still there as well. For some reason I forgot it."

"Good, and my suggestion to you is to forget about the plan. Don't even worry about it, or any of Kara's things. Leave them as they are, and give yourself more time before you try to do anything. Don't make any plans for any of it either, just wing it."

"Really, you think so?"

"Yes Mark, yes I do. You've been through a lot in the past two years, and you need to give yourself more time to heal. Jumping right in and forcing yourself to heal is never a good idea. Try and slow down, and you'll find in time, when you're ready, you'll be able to move ahead. For now, just take it as easy as you can, if you want to do something that's within reason, do it. If you don't, don't. No pressure. Take things as slowly as you can."

"Oh trust me, I'm gonna try to."

"Good, now let me ask you. Has this been the only time in your life that you've had suicidal thoughts, or attempted it?"

"Yeah it is."

"Are you sure Mark?"

"Oh yeah, I'm positive. Up until recently, I've never even remotely thought about it."

"Have you since tried, or thought about it?"

"No, not at all. In fact, the attempt I made scared me so much, that I don't think the thought of it will ever cross my mind again."

"Okay, now what if it does?"

"I immediately call your hotline."

"Very good. Now how about your work, whats going on with that?"

"I haven't even bothered with work. Hell, I haven't even been home yet to check my messages, which is something I should do, but I really still don't wanna go back to that house."

"Well if you don't want to, then don't."

"I really should though, even though I told everyone I'd be back in two weeks, I bet my phone's been burning up anyways. I keep that one separate from my car phone; only a handful of people have that number, I could have been checking my messages from that one while I was gone, but I didn't want to, but now I'm kind of interested in seeing who's called."

"Well then, maybe you should."

"Maybe? I don't know, I'm not really quite sure."

"Well, remember like I said, if you're not sure, don't force yourself right now to do anything. Just take your time, and you'll know when the time's right."

"Yeah, hopefully."

"Trust me, you will, and as each day goes by, you should start feeling less and less confused. And I say confused, because I'm sensing some confusion from you. Are you feeling confused Mark?"

"Yeah somewhat." Mark somberly replied.

"Is it bad?"

"Sort of. I mean it comes and goes."

"Well, when you feel yourself starting to get confused, try and focus your mind on what makes sense to you, and for the moment, you should find that things will become clearer, and easier. But remember, for now, try and take your time with it."

"You know what? That's a good idea, and I will definitely try it."

"Good, now if you don't mind me asking…?"

"Nope, go ahead."

"You said you haven't been home. Are you staying with a friend or relative, or something?"

"I'm staying with my mother for now, plus I'm using her car until I can get back up north to get mine, which for me is a good thing, because I really don't feel like being alone."

"Yes, that is a good thing. And honestly, right now you shouldn't be alone. You'll find that sometimes being around people can help ease your pain. Um? Does your mother or anyone else know of your suicide attempt?"

"Heck no!" Mark said with excitement, "You're the only one, and I would like to keep it that way."

"Alright, for now my lips are sealed." Doctor Susan replied with a half smile, "As long as you stick to the promise you made."

"Oh trust me, I promise."

"Good. Now one more thing, and this is totally kind of off-the-wall, and off the subject."

"What's that?"

"Well, your cottage. Do you ever rent it out?"

"I've thought about it a few times… Why?"

"Well, I haven't gone away in quite awhile, plus I've always loved Northern Michigan. And I was wondering if you wouldn't mind renting it to my sister and I for a week?"

"No, not at all. As a matter of fact, you're more than welcome to. Its kind of a mess right now though, only because I left it that way. But yeah, go ahead."

"Don't worry, we'll take care of everything."

"Cool!" Mark said while he sat up and thought as he took notice to the fact that Doctor Susan had quickly glanced at her watch, *Hmm, it must already be that time...*

"So, how much for seven days?" Doctor Susan asked.

"Oh no, no way, I'm not gonna charge you anything."

"Oh come on, I insist."

"No really, you don't understand, I already have so much money that I don't know what to do with it, and I don't need anymore."

"Are you sure Mark?"

"Trust me, I'm positive."

"Okay then, it's settled. Now all I need is an address."

Spinning around in her chair, Doctor Susan grabbed a pen, and a pad of paper from her desk, then turned back around and handed them both to Mark.

Mark wrote down the street and address, and said as he handed the pen and paper back to Doctor Susan, "The front door key is under the Indian statue in the front yard, you'll know it when you see it. I'll call and let the one neighbor that's there all year around know that you'll be there. Leave the furnace on sixty-five degrees when you leave, and make sure you both have fun."

"Okay, will do, and thank you."

"No, thank you, and I'll see you in what, eight days?"

"Yes, and remember, in the meantime, if you need anything, you can call my hotline."

"Okay, and thanks again."

"You bet, and you can close the door this time if you don't mind."

"Nope, not at all. I'll be seeing you."

"K thanks, and Mark, have a good afternoon."

"You too."

Mark then left, and Doctor Susan sat silent for a moment and just stared at the wall; she stared for quite some time.

Soon twenty minutes had gone by, and she didn't even notice, she just kept staring; she was momentarily catatonic.

Ten more minutes went by…

She snapped out of it and thought, What the hell is it about him that's so different? Man it's driving me nuts. You know you should just forget about it before it makes you insane. True, but still… Fuck it!

Someone then knocked on her door and startled her, *Shit! Scare me half to death!*

They knocked again, it was a female office assistant, "Doctor Susan?"

Doctor Susan ignored her…

She knocked again, "Doctor Susan."

"Yeah?" Doctor Susan finally answered as she stood up, mumbled, "Fucking bitch, what the fuck does she want?" She went and opened the door, "What's up?"

"Um, you have another appointment, and they've been waiting a half an hour. Um, is everything okay?"

"Yeah everything's fine. Why?"

"I, uh, well you're usually more punctual, and I just wanted to see if you were alright."

"Well thanks for your concern, but I'm fine."

"Okay, well would you like me to send them back.?"

"No, I'll go and call them back."

"Okay."

The assistant then walked off while Doctor Susan went to call her next appointment and thought, *Stupid fucking bitch! Are you all right? Yeah, I'm just fucking peachy! Moron!*

24

A few days after Mark had gone back to see Doctor Susan, his mother convinced him that he should try to go home for a little bit, and he did, but he didn't stay long. He only went in long enough to take a quick walk through and grab his phone and a few clothes. Mark didn't want to be there any longer then he had to be, it still hurt to much to be there, and it was just to empty feeling. There was nothing there for him anymore, and there probably never would be again. He just didn't want it anymore, and when he left, he drove away thinking, *I wonder if after I get a few things out of there that I want, if I could just donate the whole damn house with everything in it? Hmm, don't know? I'm gonna find out though. I think I'll let Kara's mom come and get all of Kara's things first. As for me, all I need is the rest of my clothes, all of my work stuff, and a few family heirlooms. After that, the rest can all go with the house. In the meantime, I should probably find an apartment for awhile, cause I've gotta be driving my mother nuts. I should probably pick up another car as well. She'd probably like her's back, and I have no clue as to when I'll be back to the cottage to get mine. Hmm, sounds like a plan. Remember though, like Doctor Susan said, take your time, you don't want to relapse.*

Mark stopped at a restaurant to eat while he was out…

While he was there he checked his messages, and to his surprise, he only had one. One full one, the rest were all hang-ups. Obviously everyone took his message seriously. But now that it had been about two weeks, Mark figured he had better change it, and start talking to people again. Which he did after he ate and listened to the one message that was left.

The message was from his publishing company, it was Andrea, She said, "Hi Mark, it's Andrea. I know this is a bad time for you, and I'm so, so sorry for your loss. I sincerely hope things are going well for you, and I know you're going to be gone for two weeks. Hey, that's really understandable, we all sometimes need time to get our heads straight; I sure know I would, and have. So take your time and don't hurry, and when you get time, or get back, would you please give me a call? It's very important. Thank you, and again, I'm sorry for your recent loss. Goodbye, and have a nice day…"

Mark then changed his message to, "Hi it's Mark, I'm back now, so leave me a message, and when I get a chance, I'll get back with you. Thanks and goodbye."

Mark got up, paid his bill, and left the restaurant. He spent the rest of the day car shopping, which was something he really enjoyed, and for a short while it even helped him to let go a little. It just took him awhile to find a car that he liked.

At the end of the day, and after he had finally found and bought a car, Mark even called Andrea back, plus he had also started to think about his work again.

He was healing, and his wounds were beginning to close…

25

Session Seven

A few days later in Doctor Susan's office, Mark, feeling quite a bit better about things, and not having to many negative thoughts, sat patiently waiting for Doctor Susan to enter the room, and thought about how this session might go. He also wondered how her trip to the cottage went. He hoped that she'd had fun. *If she had even went?* Mark thought, *More then likely she did though, she seemed to be really enthused about going...*

Mark's thoughts turned for a moment to the house that he didn't want anymore...

Then Doctor Susan walked in, shut the door behind her, and said, "Hello," as she went to her chair and sat down. Smiling, she asked, "So, how you doing today, anything new since our last visit?"

"I'm alright, and yeah, actually quite a few things are new." Mark replied.

"Like what?" Doctor Susan asked with a warm smile.

"Well I bought a new car, I got myself an apartment, I haven't got rid of the house or anything in it yet. Still don't feel like it, and I supposedly won another writer's award, which is being presented to me at some convention in New York tomorrow. My plane leaves tonight."

"Really Mark? Why that's great!"

"Yeah, maybe…" Mark somberly said.

"Maybe? You don't sound to thrilled." Doctor Susan asked with a look of concern.

"Well I' am a little," Mark replied, "but not really. I mean, it's not my first award, and in light of recent events, I sort of have a hard time being thrilled about really anything. Don't get me wrong, I am extremely grateful. I've just developed a strange kind of phobia towards getting happy when something good comes along. I mean, I try, but trying really doesn't work. It's like I've got this thing in my head saying, why be happy or excited about something? It's not going to last, and something shitty that's gonna cause you a lot of grief is gonna happen. So why get happy and excited, or look forward to really anything? And you know, now that I think of it, it really hasn't been recently that I've felt that way about things. If I look back, even as far back as my childhood, I pretty much on and off have always felt that way for most of my life."

"Why do you think that is?"

"Well, because it seems like anytime anything good happens, the double, triple, quadruple amount of bad is right around the corner. You can call me a whiner, but I believe that's true. It's crazy I know, but my mind, especially lately, has been programmed to expect the bad and to only look at things in a negative way. But at least I'm functioning, and I no longer wanna kill myself. Nor will I probably ever."

"Well that's good," Doctor Susan said as she spoke with her hands, "and in light of recent events, it is understandable that you feel that way. You have been through a lot, and over time those feelings should go away. But if you've been feeling like that your whole life, well then there might be a deeper problem.

Now tell me, when you feel that way, is it something that's constantly there, or is it sometimes there and sometimes not?"

"Sometimes there, sometimes not." Mark replied as he cleared his throat, "It comes and goes, and its mainly when something good is about to take place. Its rarely when things are running at a normal pace."

"Are the feelings ever overwhelming? I mean like, um… Do they ever stop you from functioning?"

"No, they don't stop me from functioning. But they do sometimes make me feel like I'm losing my mind. Especially lately. Its like there's a screaming match between me and something else that lives in my head, and it just keeps going, and going. You know, I loved my wife. I loved her more than myself sometimes. I also loved my uncle. I loved him more than I would ever be able to explain to anyone. And I'm very grateful that the both of them were in my life. And I really do think it sucks that they died, and my unborn daughter. I mean I really do, but I wanna move on with my life. I don't wanna live in it anymore, but man, if my mind that's full of racing thoughts now all the fucking time, won't shut up, I don't think I'll be able to."

"Is it that bad?" Doctor Susan asked as she leaned back in her chair.

"Oh yeah, sometimes. Sometimes it's really bad." Mark replied.

"Along with the racing thoughts, are you experiencing major mood swings too?"

"No, not really. I'm just basically tired of shit going wrong, and I'm tired of always expecting something to go wrong. You know, I have to be the most unlucky miserable millionaire on the planet."

"Hmm, I wouldn't be so sure about that?"

"Really?" Mark asked with a voice full of surprise.

"Oh yeah, trust me there are others," Doctor Susan replied with an assuring tone, "and I don't think it's the fact that you're miserable, I think you're just a man who's recently been through a lot, and hasn't had enough time to heal."

"You think?"

"Yes Mark, I do, and what you have to realize is, and what you need to force yourself to understand, no matter how hard it seems, is these kind of things take time. For some it can take years. For others it can take a lifetime."

"A lifetime, you're kidding?"

"No Mark, I'm not."

"Well I sure as hell don't wanna spend the rest of my life feeling like this."

"Then don't."

"Yeah, like it can be that simple."

"Well, if you want it to be, it can."

"How do you figure?"

"Well you said yourself that you wanna move on and stop feeling the way you do."

"Yeah?"

"Well, if you truly want to, then you will. The only way you won't, is if there's a part of you that doesn't."

"I don't get it?" Mark said with some confusion.

Doctor Susan replied, "Think about it like this; most people generally try to avoid things they don't want to do, and generally, within reason, people will usually do what they truly want."

"Oh, so what you're saying, is if I really want to move forward, then I will?"

"Exactly. But remember Mark, there is nothing wrong with reflecting. As long as it's in a positive way. And also remember to tell yourself, you can still hang on, just not too tight."

"I'll try and remember that."

"Good. Now your racing thoughts; and again you're probably experiencing them due to everything you've recently experienced, and they should fade with time. However if they don't, and they become to overwhelming, then we should probably do a deeper e-val, and discuss what meds maybe suitable for you."

"Meds, yeah, that's something I would like to try and avoid. Like I said before, I've seen that type of thing make a lot of people worse then they already are."

"Hmm," Doctor Susan thought for a moment, "maybe for some that's true, and its usually because they don't stick with the right regimen. As for you, I don't think that would be the case, and I also don't think we'll have to go that route."

"No?" Mark asked.

"No," Doctor Susan replied, "I don't. I only suggested it as a just in case, you know, a last resort."

"Yeah, one that's hopefully light years away."

"Hopefully yes it will be. Just tell yourself that."

"I will, and I think I should start working out again. That used to always make me feel better. When Kara passed, and I had moved on from my uncle, I majorly slacked off. In fact, I stopped altogether."

"Yes then," Doctor Susan said with a smile, "if it makes you feel better, then definitely start again. A good jolt of dopamine never hurt anyone."

"Dopamine?" Mark asked with a weird look.

"Yes, Dopamine." Doctor Susan replied again with a smile, "It's one of our bodies natural, "feel good," drugs, and for most of us, a good workout usually causes the brain to produce and release a good sized amount of it."

"Ah, yeah I forgot about that, and so that's why after I cool down from a workout I feel so good."

"Yep, that's exactly why. Good levels of dopamine can also help with clearer thinking."

"You know, as a matter of fact, I do think more clearly after a workout, and my mind also tends to slow down."

"Well Mark, there you go. If it helps, then do it."

"Oh I will."

"Good, and also try some deep breathing techniques when you feel your mind is starting to race. Plus, if you don't mind me asking…?"

"No, not at all." Mark replied.

"Do you belong to a church, or practice a religion, or something of that nature?"

"No, not really. I mean, I have my own spiritual beliefs that are very personal to me, but no, no church, and no religion. To me, that kind of thing is pretty much a controlling mental fairy tale."

"Wow Mark, I've never heard it put that way."

"Sorry, but to me that's the truth. Plus man, it's always the same old bullshit stories, good versus evil, and puny little humanity is caught up in the middle of the whole thing. Really? Come on, give me a break. It's all a farce. Excuse me. But if I may?"

"No, go ahead." Doctor Susan said with enthusiasm. She was really interested in what Mark had to say, and she thought it just might make it clear to her what she felt was so different about him.

"Well," Mark replied, "there's billions and billions of stars, galaxies, and planets throughout this whole massive universe we live in, you know damn well we're not the only so-called intelligent beings there are, if you think we are, well then you're stupid, and yet we're so special that God, and Satan are only walking among us fighting some kind of war, yeah sure. Humans have wonderful imaginations, but I think it's time we all evolved out of believing in wives tales and got to something more real. I will say this though, if God and Satan are real, why are we caught up in the middle of their fight? Just like our stupid leaders here on earth, they should just put on the gloves, duke it out, have a pissing and moaning contest, and leave us the fuck out if it."

"Really? Wow, that's a pretty strong view Mark."

"Yeah it is, and I'm sorry you had to hear my crap, I can sometimes get a little carried away, especially on the subject of religion."

"No, don't be sorry. That was actually a very interesting viewpoint."

"Really, well thanks. Most people get pissed off at me for my views. That's why I just usually keep my mouth shut."

"I'm a doctor, Mark, I'm supposed to be subjective."

"Yeah, I forgot that part… You know, I'll tell you something, then I'll leave it alone. That's if you don't mind?"

"No, not at all, shoot."

"In my opinion, again, if God and Satan are real, which I highly doubt they are, they're both full of shit, and Earth would be better off without them."

"Wow Mark, that's deep." Doctor Susan said, and thought at the same time, Okay, now I know what's different about this guy. He thinks in ways that I've never imagined one could think, or heard anyone else put it. Thank god I finally know.

"Well, that's what I think. I think they're both full of shit, and if they are real, again, why do we have to be in the middle of their crap? I mean come on, someone took a bite of a piece of fruit, and I've got to pay for it. Why, I didn't do it?"

"Good point."

"Anyways, I'll shut up. I'm sure you don't wanna hear it."

"Nope, I don't mind at all. I don't think we have enough time though. Maybe next session." Doctor Susan said as she glanced at her watch.

Mark replied as he thought again, *Must be time to go?* "Yeah maybe, or maybe I'll write a book on the subject, and then you can just read about it."

"Maybe, and you know if you feel that strongly, then maybe you should?"

"Maybe, but I'd hate to start a war."

"Why would you start a war?"

"Come on, the minute anyone writes about, or talks down any part of any kind of religion, it always starts some kind of fight, big or small, and I've spent to much of my life fighting with people, so maybe I shouldn't."

"Good point. But just because you write it, that doesn't mean you have to have it published."

"Yeah, that's true. You know, I could just make something like that my personnel journal? Hmm, yeah, I think I'll do that. Maybe someone will find it after I'm dead and make a million?"

"Yeah, you never know, anythings possible."

"Well somethings are, not everything. I can't get my wife back."

"No Mark, you can't, but you will always have her memory, and in time, you should find that because you'll always have her memory, that she'll always be a part of you."

"Yeah I know, and thanks for the reminder."

"You bet."

"Okay then. I guess it's see you again in a week?"

"No, actually if you don't mind?" Doctor Susan said as she thought for a moment, "I'd like to see you again in three days."

"Um yeah, okay, that's fine with me." Mark replied as he stood up off from the couch and stretched his back.

"Okay, just let the secretary know, and I'll see you then."

"Alright, will do… Oh wait a minute…"

"What's up?"

"Did you and your sister have fun up north, or did you even go?"

"Yes we went, and yes, we had a wonderful time. That's a very nice place you have there, you're a lucky man, and I'm sorry I didn't say anything, I was meaning to tell you, and also tell you thanks, but we got to talking and it totally slipped my mind."

"No that's cool, I'm glad you had fun. I just hope you didn't mind the mess?"

"Nope, not at all... And, I hope you don't mind, but we cleaned and straightened everything up for you?"

"Nope, don't mind a bit. Actually, I really appreciate it."

"I kind of figured you would. Hmm, we even put the key back under the Indian statue, and left the furnace on sixty-five like you asked."

"Cool, thanks." Mark said with a smile.

"You're very welcome," Doctor Susan warmly replied, "and thank you, and I'll see you in three days."

"Alright, I'll see you then."

"Bye."

26

A few hours after his session with Doctor Susan, Mark's plane arrived in New York City. Shortly after, he caught a cab, rode from the airport to a nice high-rise hotel, then checked in, and found his way to his room. Fortunately for Mark, the convention he was to attend the next day was in the same building, so he didn't have to venture very far, which was something Mark didn't like to do when he wasn't close to home. So, after he got settled in, Mark ordered room service and pretty much stayed in his room. He brought the rough draft of the manuscript he had started before Kara died, he had planned on trying to do some work on it, but when he tried, he just couldn't do it, he kept drawing a blank. Nothing would come to him, and it just didn't seem to matter. He couldn't focus, and he'd also been feeling angry for some reason. Ever since he arrived in New York he felt that way. Why he did? Mark had no idea, he just did. Plus he really didn't even want to be where he was. Nor did he really even want to go to the award ceremony. *What's the use?* Mark thought, *I'd rather be at the cottage.* So Mark said, "Screw the manuscript, I'll work on it another time." He then tossed it to the side, flipped on the television, and sat watching it until he fell asleep.

Getting up early the next day to a wake-up call, Mark slowly rose, and gradually got ready to go to the award ceremony, which he still really didn't want to go to, but he knew he had to, so later in the day, still feeling angry for some reason, he went. He didn't have any fun. He just faked his way through the whole thing, and the whole time all he could think was, *I can't wait til this is fucking over with!*

27

Two hours after the awards ceremony and the banquet that followed was over, Mark found himself sitting alone in the hotel's bar. Still feeling angry, and also sadly missing Kara's warm company, Mark ordered himself a mixed drink, bought a pack of cigarettes, and decided he was going to sit and get as drunk as he possibly could. *Fuck it!* Mark thought, *What else is there to do? Nothing. So I'm gonna get numb. Maybe I'll even start a fight with someone? Yeah, that sounds like a good idea. Naw, I'd better not. Knowing my luck I'd get my ass kicked. Hmm? You never know though, I might win? Yeah, we'll see...?*

Mark guzzled his drink, and asked the bartender for another, which as soon as he got, he guzzled as well, and immediately asked for another; he guzzled that one too.

He repeated it several more times...

He was on a mission...

By the time he had got his seventh drink, he had smoked over a half a pack of cigarettes, and he was starting to feel really drunk, which only amplified the anger he was feeling, and he kept stewing in it for some reason. *Nothing,* Mark thought, *would ever make him happy again. Why? What's the purpose of really anything? Nothing. Right? And everything's wrong. Why? Fuck this place and everything in it! And fuck that guy at the end of the bar! Who's he, and whats he looking at? Cocksucker! Fuck the bartender too! Fucking bald-headed Irish-looking prick! Motherfucker can't even mix a good drink. How did that Jew fuck get this job anyways? Goofy-looking mother fucker! Oh, and look at that cunt fucking waitress. I wonder what stinking fuck-hole she crawled out of? Stupid looking cum-trap. The best pieces of her probably ran down her mother's fucking leg. Dumb-ass slime ball bitch! Man I've gotta piss. Where's the bathroom? Ah, there it is.*

With those thoughts still going through his head, Mark got up and made his way to the bathroom, and took care of his business.

After, he came back to the bar, Mark sat down, guzzled the rest of his drink, and ordered another. Only this time he asked for a double, which he got and guzzled as well.

Now feeling extremely drunk, Mark ordered another double, but this time he didn't guzzle it. Instead, he took his time with it. Feeling as drunk as he felt, Mark had thought he had better try and slow down.

Forty-five minutes later, Mark was totally wasted. In fact, he was so wasted, when he went to order another drink, he spoke in almost complete gibberish, which sounded normal to him, but not to the bartender. To him it sounded like a bunch of jumbled up mumbling, sort of like low baby talk, and so he cut Mark off. He was to drunk for another drink.

Mark didn't think so though. So he proceeded to drunkenly argue with the bartender, which made absolutely no sense, because the bartender had already made up his mind, and he really couldn't understand much of what Mark was saying anyway. So in the end, after the bartender threatened to call hotel security, and Mark managed to call him a, "Bald Headed Irish Fucking Prick!" He lost the argument, paid his tab, grabbed what was left of his smokes, staggered out of the bar, and off to his room.

Eventually reaching his room, Mark stumbled around while

he opened the door.

Quickly staggering in, Mark slammed the door behind him, stumbled sloppily across the room, tripped over his own feet, smacked his forehead on the corner of a wooden nightstand, and wiped out a lamp as he recklessly fell to the floor.

The impact with the table knocked him out cold.

Fifteen hours later, Mark woke up with a massive bump on his head, and a horrific headache.

28

Session Eight

While Mark laid knocked out on the floor of his hotel room, he had a very deep dream. A dream that every time he thought about it, gave him warm goose bumps, and made him feel whole again. His grieving, because of the dream, would now finally be over. In it, while Mark stood on the beach of their Thunder Bay cottage and gazed up at the star filled Milky Way sky, Kara came to him. Dressed in her favorite purple summer gown, she mystically formed out of the misty darkness of a moonlit night, and walked to him. She put her arms around him. Mark could smell her perfume, he could feel her soft warm skin, he could feel her heart beating, he could feel the air around him, waves gently rolled across the lake top, they had a calm, serene sound to them. Kara's hair was so soft-looking, her eyes so beautifully deep with compassion, to Mark she looked like an angel. An angel that had come to calm his weary soul. She kissed him. He kissed her. They held each other tight. He ran his fingers through her hair, she rubbed his cheek, they kissed again. Kara looked passionately into her lover's eyes and softly spoke to him. She said, "Mark my love, it's time to move on."

"I can't." He replied.

"Please Mark, move on for me."

They kissed again…

"Please," Kara said again, "I love you oh so much, and I want you to be happy again. So please, for me and our love. Let go and live again. Don't let the sadness you feel ruin you. Please, if anything, do it for me, and I promise part of me will always be with you."

"Promise?"

"Yes my love, I promise. Now go and live, and I'll always be here with you."

They passionately kissed and hugged again, and Kara then let go and slowly vanished back into the dark mist.

"I'll always remember you," Mark whispered, "I'll never forget."

He then woke up, and besides the throbbing bump on his head, and the hangover he had, Mark felt pretty good about life again. The dream made him feel like a new man. He wanted to live again, and he wanted to live life to its fullest. *No more confusion, no more sadness. It was time to start a new and leave everything behind.* That's what he thought when he woke up, and that's what he thought while he waited for Doctor Susan to step into her office. The positive outlook didn't fade, and Mark, under no circumstances was ever going to let it fade. For his love of Kara, and in her honor, he was going to do exactly what she, in the dream had asked him to do. He felt so relieved, it was like a big emotional knot that had been tightly tied around his heart had finally come completely undone. It felt good, and he felt good.

Doctor Susan stepped into the room, shut the door behind her, and said as she went and sat in her chair, "Well hello Mark." She smiled at him and asked, "How are you?"

"Good, yourself?" Mark replied.

"I'm doing alright."

"That's good."

"So how was your trip?"

"It was okay."

"Just okay?"

"Yeah, it was pretty much like all the rest. Arrive, check in, lounge around, meet and greet people, shake hands and say thanks, go back to my room, lounge around again, checkout, then go home. So it was just okay."

"Nothing exciting happened?"

"Um... No, not really." Mark replied and said with a half-smile, "Well if you consider me getting really drunk after the award banquet exciting. Then maybe, yeah something exciting happened. But other than that, no, not really."

"Really drunk huh?" Doctor Susan asked, "Why did you do that, were you celebrating?" Inside, She thought that Mark getting drunk was kind of funny, and she tried not to laugh or show it. She didn't want him to know that's what she thought.

Mark replied, "No, not at all, and in all actuality I didn't even wanna be there. I can't explain why I didn't either. I just didn't. Plus, from the time I had left home, up until the day after the banquet, I felt really mad. Not just irritation either, I mean I felt pissed. Why? I had and have no clue? I just did. So after everything that day was said and done, I decided I was gonna have a few drinks. I thought it would change my mood. Boy that was a mistake."

"It only made your mood worse didn't it?"

"Oh yeah, it sure did."

"Most times you'll find that in most people, alcohol will usually only intensify the mood you're in. So if you're already feeling mad at something, then it's usually best not to drink at all."

"Oh trust me, I know that now, and I sort of found it out the hard way."

"How so, what happened?" Doctor Susan asked as she still kept her laughter to herself.

Mark replied with another half grin. "Well besides getting totally annihilated, if my memory serves me right, I gave the bartender a pretty hard time when he cut me off."

"Wow! You got that bad that you got cut off?"

"Oh yeah, I sure did. Like I said, I got annihilated, and I got that way really quick, and when that guy cut me off, whew man! Lets just say it got bad. It's probably a good thing he did though, because there's no telling what would have happened if he didn't. Hmm? I just hope he doesn't remember me."

"Yeah, no kidding. I'm sure you're good though. It was a bar, and I'm pretty sure that kind of thing happens all the time." Doctor Susan said as she laughed even harder on the inside, and remembered what had happened on the night her and her husband went out.

"Yeah that's true," Mark replied, "but I do kind of still feel stupid about it."

"Well by chance, if you're ever there again, make it a point to apologize to the guy or something."

"Yeah, that sounds like a real good idea. Of course that's if the place would even let me in."

"Oh I'm sure they will."

"Yeah maybe? Who knows though? I'll just have to wait and see."

"Yeah, there you go. Just remember, if you're feeling any

anger, don't order a drink."

Mark then laughed and said as Doctor Susan also laughed, "Oh believe me I won't."

Doctor Susan then said, "Good. Now could you tell me why you were feeling angry, or you still don't know?"

"I have no clue as to why. I mean like I said before, I just was."

"Do you think maybe you're still grieving, and that's what's causing you to feel certain ways without you really even knowing why?"

"Yeah, probably then, but not now."

"Probably then, but not now? Why do you say that?" Doctor Susan asked with a curious tone.

"Well," Mark replied, "because then I was still grieving, and you're right, that's probably the reason I felt the unexplained anger. But now there's no more anger, and believe it or not, I'm not grieving anymore. And I'm not going to, and nor do I want to."

"Well that's good, because grief is usually never a positive force. Hmm? So what changed? Um, why do you feel the way you do now as compared to how you felt only a few days ago?"

"Well, the night I got drunk, after I was cut off, I went back to my room, I went in, I tripped over my own feet, I fell, I bashed my forehead on the corner of an end table on the way down. That's how I got this lump."

"I was gonna ask you about that."

"Yeah it's embarrassing looking isn't it?"

"No, not really."

"Hmm, thanks."

"Welcome."

"Anyways, the impact with the table knocked me clean out."

"Ouch! That had to have hurt."

"Yeah, tell me about it. When I came to, I had the worst headache you could have imagined."

"I bet. You're lucky it didn't kill you."

"Oh yeah I know, that combined with the amount of booze I drank, I'm surprised it didn't, and even though at the time I felt like I wanted to die, I'm glad I didn't. And I'm also glad it happened. If I had to, I would gladly do it all over again."

"Really? No kidding, why's that?" Doctor Susan asked as her stomach began to hurt again, *Shit!* She thought, *Not again…*

Mark replied, "Oh yeah, I really would. And the reason is because of the dream I had while I was unconscious."

"Wow. So what happened in the dream?"

"You know it's really personal and I would rather not share it at this moment. Hmm? Well okay, lets just say I had an epiphany that totally changed the way I feel."

"Okay if you don't want to, you don't have to, and for now we'll just leave it at that. However, if you want to share it later on, you will be more then welcome to."

"Oh trust me, if I think there's gonna be a need to, I will."

"Good."

"Honestly though, I don't think I'm gonna have to."

"That's okay too. We'll let you decide if and when the time is right. If you change your mind at anytime, I'll be here."

"Yeah I know, and thanks."

"You bet. That's what I'm here for, and as long as you're feeling good, it makes me feel good. You are feeling good, right?"

"Yeah, I'm feeling better then I've felt in a long time, and it's going to stay that way."

"Good then, I'll see you next time in two weeks. That's unless you think you'll need to come back sooner?"

"No, I'm good."

"Okay then, two weeks from now, and remember if you need anything, feel free to call my hotline."

"Oh I will, and thanks again."

"You're welcome."

29

Session Nine

"Well Mark, it's been two weeks since the last time we spoke. How are you doing, things are going well I hope?"

"Yeah, things are going good." Mark replied to Doctor Susan as she stepped into the room and sat in her chair, "I haven't felt depressed, and I haven't felt any anxiety or deep sadness."

"Good. How about any thoughts of suicide, have you been having those at all?"

"Nope, not at all."

"Good, that's great to hear. Um? So what have you been doing with yourself? You haven't been out harassing bartenders have you?"

"Ah ha ha ha!" Mark laughed and said, "No I haven't. It sounds like a good idea though."

"Really?" Doctor Susan laughed.

"No, just kidding. Um, I've just mainly been working on a book. By the way it's almost done."

"Wow! That's great!"

"Yeah it is, and I appreciate your enthusiasm. I just hope my publisher and the public feels the same way."

"Oh I'm sure it'll go over well."

"Hmm… Maybe. I don't know, we'll just have to wait and see. Anyways, I've been doing that, and I've also been making preparations to donate Kara's and my house with everything in it to this local housing organization that helps put low-income families into nice houses."

"Really Mark, that's great. If you don't mind me asking though...?"

"No not at all."

"What made you decide to do that?"

"I just simply don't want the house, and nor do I wanna be there, and even though I'm keeping a few personal items from it. I just simply don't want anything that's there either. It's all just to empty now. Plus I wanna live up north at my cottage. Which is something I've wanted to do since Kara and I bought it. So now that I can, why not?"

"Are you sure there's not part of you that's still just trying to run from your memories? Because you know, if there is a part of you that is, moving away might do more harm then good."

"Yeah I'm sure there's not, and you know I did think about that being the case, and in the beginning it was. But now I assure you it's not. It's just something I've always wanted to do, and now that I have the chance to, I'm going to. I've always wanted to learn to fly a plane as well, and once I get settled there, I'm gonna also start my small craft pilot training."

"Now that sounds like fun." Doctor Susan said with a smile, "I've always wanted to learn to fly myself. I've just never been able to find the time for it."

Mark replied, "Well maybe you should make time."

"Yeah maybe I should. We'll see though, it is quite expensive."

"Yeah that it is, but now that I have the money, and plenty of it, I'm gonna go for it."

"That's good, and if that's what you want, then you should definitely go for it."

"Oh yeah, most definitely. And you know, after I'm done, I'm thinking about possibly opening a small chartering service. Of course though, if my books are keeping me to busy, other people would have to run it while I'm away, or something. I don't know."

"Well that sounds like a good plan. Setting goals is always a good thing, and I sincerely hope you reach them."

"Yeah, me too."

"Just remember Mark, be optimistic, roll with the punches, and I'm sure you will."

"Optimism? Now there's something I haven't felt in a long time."

"But you are now, right?"

"Yeah, more than I used to."

"Good, that's great to hear. Now how do you personally feel about your sessions? Do you feel they've been helpful?"

"Oh yeah, more than you know."

"Okay good. Now from this point on, do you feel you need more?"

"Hmm? That's a tough question to answer. Hmm? Well… At this point I'd like to say no, I don't need anymore. But just in case something comes up, I would probably say it would be a good idea if we could leave the door open. You know, just in case."

"Okay then, that's what we'll do. We'll leave the door open, and I won't close your case, and I'll leave it up to you to schedule more sessions, if in the future you feel you need them. Plus remember, you can always also for any reason, if you feel the need, call my hotline."

"Oh trust me, if I need to, I won't hesitate."

"Good, I'm glad to hear it, and okay, if there's not really a reason to be here right now. Is there?"

"No, I don't think so."

"Okay then, you obviously won't object to us cutting out early."

"Nope, not at all."

"Alright then, you take care, and good luck with all of your endeavors, and hopefully we'll meet again under different circumstances."

"Yeah no kidding, and thanks. Thanks again for everything."

"You bet... Oh, and by the way. You or your insurance, whichever won't be charged for today or your last session. It's on me."

"Cool, thanks. But you really don't have to."

"Naw come on, they were only a half session apiece. It wouldn't be fair for me to charge. Plus it's the least I could do for you, for you letting my sister and I stay at your cottage. Which by the way again, is a very beautiful place. I can see why you're going to move there. I would too, if I were you."

"Really? Well thanks."

"Oh yeah, most definitely."

"Wow, cool, and thanks again, and maybe I'll see you some time."

"Okay. Bye now, and good luck."

"Yep, and thanks."

30

Shortly after her session with Mark, Doctor Susan left her office early and went home. She wasn't feeling well. For some reason her mysterious stomachache was back, she felt shaky from the inside out, and her thoughts kept dwelling on her deceased husband. Why she was feeling this way, she had no clue. It was like an emotional time bomb had blown up inside of her, and it had begun to quickly poison her whole body with overbearing grief. She felt just awful, and it wasn't the flu. Why? What triggered it? She had been doing so well for so long. Why now? She had no clue, and she was sick.

At home, after she went in, she panicked, her heart raced, she looked around her big empty house, and felt total emptiness. She couldn't bear it, and total insanity began to fall in all around her. It consumed her. She began to breath heavily. She got tunnel vision. She began to profusely sweat. Feeling nauseated, she ran to the bathroom and threw up while she pissed herself.

She then threw up and pissed herself again, and began to cry. She cried really, really hard, and she frantically pulled at her hair, then wildly bashed her face. She broke her glasses off, tossed them against the wall, and tried to pull herself together, but she couldn't do it. She just kept crying and crying, and bashing herself. She also cussed loudly, "Fuck! Fuck you! You Goddamn Mother Fucking Cocksucker! I Fucking Hate You! You Fucking, NO GOOD FUCKING, Shit For Fucking Brains! Bitching Fucking Cunt!" She also frantically ripped all of her clothes off while she violently tossed them about the bathroom and spit at everything around her, "Fuck! Fuck you! You Goddamn Mother Fucking Cocksucker! I Fucking Hate You! You Fucking, NO GOOD FUCKING, Shit For Fucking Brains! Bitching Fucking Cunt!" She kept viciously yelling.

She went silent, and stood and looked at her face in the bathroom's vanity mirror. She studied it and laughed, then she frowned and said while she stood naked, "Maybe it's time the counselor gets some counseling herself?" She then wildly screamed at her reflection while she squeezed both of her breast together so hard that they deeply bruised, "YOU STUPID FUCKING CUNT! YEAH SURE! OHH! OHH! FUCK ME! FUCK ME! COME ON, YOU WANNA FUCK ME!? YOU DUMB FUCKING BITCH!" She then quickly without thinking, bashed her reflection with the side of her fist, and smashed the mirror to pieces, which also cut her hand in the process, and was now bleeding pretty bad.

She ran out of the bathroom, made her way into the kitchen, and madly danced about it. Like a psychotic loony, she wildly flung herself around the room, scattered everywhere the blood from her bleeding hand, bashed herself into the walls, smeared the blood all over her face and ass, and hysterically laughed the whole time.

She threw herself face-down on the floor, bounced her hips up and down, made deep eerie moaning sounds, and convulsively dry humped the floor. Just like a dirty dog in heat, she crazily bashed her soft mound of flesh against the hard floor, and at the same time, with both hands ran underneath, she manually stimulated herself until she was satisfied.

After she wildly got herself off, Susan quickly got up and

A New Beginning

stood silently still while she stared at nothing.

She got herself a glass of water and sipped it while she stood naked in front of an open window.

She kept sipping and just staring. She was totally blank, and she didn't care if someone saw her.

A neighbor walked by the window.

She flipped him off and loudly cursed him as he tried not to look at her, "FUCK YOU, YOU MOTHER FUCKER! YOU NEVER SAW A PUSSY BEFORE!"

She then quickly smashed the glass of water to the floor and ran screaming through the big house, and into her bedroom.

She slammed the door behind her and stopped. She studied her body in the door's backside changing mirror for a moment. She studied her front. She laughed. She spun around, looked over her shoulder, and studied her backside. She laughed again. She spun back around, and slowly ran her hands down from her shoulders, over top of her breast, down her abdomen, and onto her pubic mound where she stopped, stared at her reflection, squeezed her mound extremely hard, slapped it, punched herself in the face, and said in a deep angry tone, "You are a dirty, dirty bitch, and you are oh so, so no good." She then screamed and wildly spit as she began to violently smash the mirror with her fist, "AND I FUCKING HATE YOU! I HATE YOU, I FUCKING HATE YOU! GODDAMN IT! GODDAMN IT! FUCK YOU, FUCK YOU! YOU MOTHER FUCKER! WHY WHY WHY!"

She kept screaming and bashing...

"FUCK YOU! FUCK! YOU FUCKING CUNT! WHY, WHY, WHY!" And she kept bashing until she totally destroyed the mirror, cried out in blood-curdling madness, collapsed to the floor from exhaustion, and passed out bleeding on the pile of broken mirror that had fallen to the floor. She hurt herself bad, and it was horrific looking. She had cuts and bruises all over her body, and for some sick and twisted reason, that's what she had wanted.

Doctor Susan had really lost it…

Why???

What was wrong with her???

Forty-eight hours later she woke up in a mental hospital, strapped down to a bed. Covered with cuts, bruises, and bandages, she slowly opened her eyes, wondered where she was, what had happened to her, and how she had gotten there. She had absolutely no clue, and it severely frightened her. Frightened her so much that she massively panicked, and a team of doctors had to rush into her room, tighten her restraints, and heavily sedate her again. She had already been sedated and heavily drugged two other times. She just kept freaking out every time she woke up, and it wasn't until two days later that she had finally woke without freaking out, and had the full realization of what was going on.

31

About five and a half months after Mark's last session with Doctor Susan, Mark was doing really well. Winter had passed in its normally slow and blustery way, the New Year came, the snow was gone, and springtime had finally arrived. The weather was getting warmer, the grass and trees were turning green again, flowers were starting to bloom, the birds were back, the bees were buzzing, the days were getting longer, and there was a general sense of newness in the air; which could be felt everywhere one went. It was Mother Nature at her true finest again. Mark had finished his book ahead of schedule, plus just like he had planned, Mark had been rid of the house for quite some time. The donation of it went really well, and it made him really happy that he got to help out a family that needed a good start. It also lifted a big load from his shoulders, and now all he had to do was see if his publisher would accept his finished work. He was pretty confident in thinking they would. Mark would then make his move to the cottage. After that, he would start his flight training, which was something that Mark was really looking forward to. He couldn't wait; he was so enthusiastic about it, that when we wasn't working on his recently-finished manuscript, that's all he could think about. Every now and then, Mark would even dream about it. This was good for him, because it meant that he was really moving forward; no more relapsing.

Everything was going so well for him, in fact things were going so good that he had mostly forgotten about all the bad that had happened. Even though every now and then he would reflect, especially on all of the good memories he had, he never lived in the bad memories of his past. Nor was he ever going to again.

Once, because of something a relative who lived out of state tried to do, Mark almost found himself falling back into the sick feelings he had, when the ordeal with his uncle was taking place. But after he sat down and wrote this relative a letter explaining in a very serious way about how he felt about her actions, he very quickly found himself feeling healthy and normal again.

The relative that never helped Mark or Kara with his uncle's business to begin with, was going to try and sue the home that he had died in, and Mark wanted nothing to do with it. Nor did he want anything, anymore, or ever again to do with the relatives that were responsible for trying to file the suit. In the letter Mark expressed that. As far as he was concerned, what was done, was done. It was his time to live, and nothing, and no one, absolutely no one, had the right to interrupt his life; especially with bullshit. Nor did they have the right to get in his way, and that's the way Mark felt then, and that's the way he feels now. To this day he still doesn't speak to the relative. Nor does he know what happened with the Law suit, and nor does he really even care.

32

One evening while Mark was slowly packing his apartment, and carefully getting things in order for his move to the cottage, he stopped and made a phone call. It was to Doctor Susan's emergency hotline, and it wasn't for an emergency. It also wasn't because he was feeling bad or down, either. It was because, for some reason he just wanted to talk to her and see how she was. He didn't know why he wanted to, he just did, and he'd been wanting to for the whole day. So after arguing with himself for quite some time, he finally did. But to his disappointment, when he finally got through, after about twenty rings, he got one of Doctor Susan's assistants. She told Mark that Doctor Susan was off on sick leave, but whatever it was that he needed, she would be glad to help him. Mark told her he really didn't need any help, but if she could get a message to Doctor Susan saying that he called for her, that it would be deeply appreciated; which the assistant agreed to do.

Two days later while Mark was still slowly packing; he'd been dragging his feet for some reason, his phone rang.

He answered it.

"Hello?" To his surprise it was Doctor Susan on the other end.

"Mark?"

"Yeah? Oh, hey, Doctor Susan! I see you got my message. How are you?"

"I'm okay. How about you?"

"I'm doing really good. In fact I'm doing great. Getting ready to move up north."

"Wow Mark that's great! I'm so happy for you."

"Thanks, I'm happy too. Been dragging my feet though."

"Why's that?"

"I don't know, just being lazy I guess. You know how moving goes, one part of you is excited to get to the new place. Then the other part just doesn't wanna work. Well at least if you're like me you don't wanna work."

"Maybe, that's a funny way to put it though."

"Yeah I guess it is. I don't know, I'm just weird like that."

"Yeah I guess. So, without sounding rude, what can I do for you? You haven't had a relapse have you?"

"No, not at all. I just wanted to see how you were."

"Gee Mark, that's thoughtful of you. It's not very often a patient wants to know how the doctor is."

"Yeah, usually it's the other way around isn't it?"

"Yeah, usually, but since you wanna know, I'm fine."

"Well that's great to hear."

"Why thank you."

"You're welcome, and now that I know that, I have one more thing to ask."

"What's that?"

"Well this may seem off the wall, and if you say, "No," I'll totally understand, and I promise I won't bother you, we'll just forget about it."

"Okay Mark, you're losing me?"

"Well I…"

"Yeah?"

"You wanna meet me for lunch sometime before I move?…

Susan, did you hang up?"

"No I didn't hang up... I. Um?... Yeah sure, I'd love to meet you for lunch. Just let me know when and where?"

"Okay, how about tomorrow, eleven thirty, at the steakhouse across from the gateway mall?"

"Sure, that sounds great."

"Okay then. Um, you do know where the place is, right?"

"Oh yeah, I know exactly where it is."

"Alright, I guess I'll see you then."

"Yep, you sure will."

"Okay great. I'll talk to you later then."

"Alright bye, and I'll see you."

"Okay, bye."

33

Waking up early the next day to his phone ringing, Mark quickly sat up in bed, grabbed the phone, looked at the LED screen to see who was calling, and then answered it, "Yeah, Andrea, it's early. What can I do for you?"

"Well, aren't we a grouchy one today?"

"I'm sorry, it's just way to early."

"To early for good news?"

"I don't know, maybe, it depends on what the good news is?"

"The good news is your manuscript has been accepted, and the president of the company was so impressed with it, that she herself personally wants us to put you on a three-month-long, all-expenses-paid book tour that would start next month and run until the end of July."

"Wow… That is good news. I think?"

"You think?"

"Just kidding. Yeah that's great."

"So I take it you're gonna be up for it?"

"Yeah, even though I'm in the process of moving right now, I'm up for it, and I'll be ready."

"Okay then, that's great. I'll be calling you sometime, and I'll also be emailing you with all the details. Sound good?"

"Yeah, sounds great."

"Okay then, bye for now."

"Bye."

Mark then hit the phone's hang up button, tossed it to the floor, and said, "SHIT! I'm going back to sleep."

Two hours later he woke up and got himself ready for his lunch date with Doctor Susan. He arrived at the restaurant a half an hour early, so he went inside, found a place to sit, ordered something to drink, and patiently waited for her to get there.

I hope she shows, Mark thought as he sat and looked around, I'll sure feel like a fool if she doesn't…

Twelve minutes later she walked in, and Mark quickly spotted her, then waved her to his table. She stepped to it with a wide smile and said, "Well hello Mark." She sat down and asked, "How are you?"

"Good." Mark replied and said as he took curious notice to her hands and face. Both hands still had bandages around them, and her left cheek had a small bruise on it, "Yourself?"

"Well considering that not to long ago I was in a pretty nasty car accident, I'm doing good."

"Wow really! That's good to hear… Well I mean, no wait. Considering that you're doing good. Not the accident. That's bad."

"Silly, I knew what you meant."

"Okay good. I'd hate to think I made it sound like the accident was good." *Boy I'm fucking stupid*, Mark then thought while Susan replied, "Nope, it didn't sound that way at all."

A waiter stopped at the table, introduced himself, and asked Susan if she would like something to drink.

She ordered a lemonade, and said to Mark, "So anyways, my car was totaled, driving a rental, and since it was the other persons fault, their insurance has to pay for everything, which includes my sick leave time."

"No kidding. Well that's good for you. Bad for the other driver though, you know their rates are probably gonna soar through the roof."

"Yeah no kidding."

The waiter came back to their table, and set Susan's drink in front of her, then said, "I'll be back in a moment to take your orders."

Mark replied, "Okay thanks."

Susan grabbed a menu and said, "Well," as she opened it, "I'd better decide. You obviously already know what you want?"

"Now why do you say that?"

"Cause you're not looking over your menu."

"Ah ha, ha, ha!" Laughed Mark. "You're right, I do already know what I want. Plus I've eaten here so often, I've got the menu memorized."

"Well I've only been here one other time, and I have no clue as to what I want. What's good?"

"The steak of course."

"Yeah I bet it is. But I'm not really hungry for steak."

"What are you hungry for?"

"Fish sounds great, and I. Oh, okay, here it is. I… Found it… Broiled Cod dinner. Mm, I know what I'm having."

The waiter came back and took their orders; first Susan's, then Mark's.

Susan said to Mark as the waiter took their menus and walked away, "So, how's the new book coming?"

"It's done?"

"Really? That's great!"

"Yeah, and my publisher has already accepted it. Plus once it goes to print, because they were so impressed with it, they're gonna be sending me on an all-expenses-paid book tour."

"Wow! That sounds exciting."

"Yeah, sort of."

"For how long?... I mean, how long is the tour gonna be?"

"Three months."

"Really."

"Yeah, it's supposed to start at the beginning of next month, and run until the end of July, but we'll see."

"What do you mean?"

"Well, things don't always go according to plan. Especially in this business."

"Yeah that's true. Life in general never usually goes according to plan."

"Boy do I know that."

The waiter brought their food to them and set it front of them. They both thought, *Wow, that was fast...*

The waiter asked before he walked away, "Okay, now can I get you two anything else?"

"Nope, it looks like we're all set." Mark and Susan both replied at the same time.

The three of them laughed for a moment, and the waiter said, "Okay then, enjoy your food, and I'll be back in awhile to check on you."

"K thanks." Susan and Mark both simultaneously replied again.

They began to eat and also carry on with small talk...

Shortly after they began eating, they were finished.

They both had full stomachs...

Mark said, "Man! That steak was good. Every time I come here is just a reminder on why I keep coming back."

"Yeah it was good. Well mine was, I don't know about yours?"

"Ah, ha, ha ha, that's funny!"

"Well I try."

The waiter came and grabbed their empty plates, and asked, "How was everything?"

Susan and Mark both replied, "Everything was delicious."

"Good, would either of you like dessert?"

Mark said, "No thanks." Then asked Susan, "How about you?"

She replied, "Nah, I'm good. But thanks for asking."

"Okay," the waiter said, "I'll be back in a moment with your bill."

Mark and Susan went back to talking...

"So Mark, I remember you were talking about donating your house to some housing organization, and since you've told me you're moving up north, obviously you've already got rid of the house, right?"

"Yeah I sure did. Why do you ask?"

"Well because I was thinking about doing the same thing with mine."

"Really, how come?"

"Well it's big, and since my husband passed, it just feels to empty."

"Boy do I know that feeling."

"I figured you would."

"Yeah no kidding... Um? Well if you're interested in donating it, I can call you later and hook you up with everything you need to know."

"Sure, that would be wonderful."

The waiter came back with their bill and said as he set it on the table, "Here you go, and if you'd like, I can take it up when you're ready?"

Mark pulled four twenties from his pocket, handed them to the waiter with the bill, and said, "Here you go, and keep the change."

"Okay, thanks, and you two have a nice day."

"You too." Susan and Mark both replied as the waiter turned and walked away.

Susan said, "You know Mark, I was more than willing to split the bill with you."

"Nah, don't worry about it. Maybe next time, how's that sound?"

"Well if you insist."

They both then stood up and made their way out of the restaurant and to the parking lot. Mark walked Susan to her car, and they continued with small talk until they got to it. When they got to it, before Susan got in, she paused and asked, "So when are you moving?"

"In a couple of days."

"Would you like some help?"

"I would love some, but I really don't need any."

"Why is that?"

"I'm having a company do it all, and all I have to do is finish packing. Hey besides, your hands don't look like they'd be up for the task."

"Yeah I know, I just thought I'd ask."

"Thanks, I appreciate it. But I've got the moving part

covered."

"Okay."

"But, if you'd like to tag along for the ride? You're more than welcome to come along."

"I'd love to."

"Okay cool. Um… I'll pick you up then. Friday morning at six. If that's okay?"

"Sure. Here now hold on."

Susan got into her car and wrote some things down onto a piece of paper.

She then rolled her window down, handed the piece of paper to Mark and said, "That's my address."

"Alright," Mark replied and said as he looked at it with a smile, "I guess I'll see you then."

"Yep, and you take care."

"Bye."

Susan started her car and drove off while Mark turned and walked away…

34

Two days after his lunch date with Susan it was Friday, and Mark got up really early, got himself ready, and went and picked her up at six like he said he would. Afterwards, he headed up to the cottage, which after a couple of stops, took about three and a half hours to get to. They didn't mind though, because it was such a beautiful, scenic ride, as it always was. The time spent was well worth it.

Some of the sights, especially the ones overlooking the mighty Lake Huron, were almost breathtaking. And add in all the freshly budding trees, and the new glowing flowers that stretched out as far as the eye could see, it all became pretty much heavenly; for the both of them it was all so tranquil, plus they really enjoyed each other's company. When they arrived at the cottage they were met in the road by the moving company, obviously they beat Mark and Susan there, and they wanted to know where to park their truck. Mark directed them to pull into the yard, and to back right up to the front door, which they did…

So the movers could get out when they were done, Mark parked his car in the road. He and Susan then got out and made small talk as they headed to the front door.

Mark unlocked the door and directed the movers to put everything in the kitchen. It was all boxes anyways. He then went inside.

With Susan following behind him, Mark made his way into the living room.

Susan went off to use the bathroom while Mark opened some curtains and gazed out at the bay for a moment.

He looked at the floor and had a flashback of what had happened the last time he was there, which was something that he had forgotten about; he didn't want to remember though, so he quickly made himself forget again. *Where was the gun though?* Mark wondered as he stared back out the window, *Susan must have done something with it when her and her sister were here… Hmm? I'll have to ask her…*

"Hey Mark." Susan called after she finished up in the bathroom and stepped out.

"Yeah?"

"I'm gonna go out to the car and get my things. Where would you like me to put them?"

"If you'd like? You can put them on the bed in the bedroom."

"K thanks."

"Do you need a hand?"

"Naw, I got it."

"Are you sure?"

"Yeah I'm sure. Thanks though."

"No problem."

Susan went out to the car…

Moments later she stepped into the living room and said while Mark turned from the window to face her, "Well, that was easy enough."

She continued with, as she stepped to the window, "What a nice day it's turning out to be. That water looks cold though."

"Yeah, that it does." Mark replied as he looked back out the window, "I don't think we'll be doing any swimming."

"Are you sure?" Susan sarcastically asked as she looked at Mark and smiled.

Their eyes met for a quick moment.

Susan tingled with emotion…

Mark replied with a laugh, "Oh yeah, I'm positive."

"Wimp."

"Wimp?"

"Just kidding."

"Yeah I know."

Susan tingled again.

Mark asked, "Um, when you and your sister were here, and you cleaned, what did you do with the gun? I mean, I kind of hope you threw it in a river or something."

"Well, I didn't throw it in a river, but I did get rid of it though."

"Really, how?"

"I sold it to a gun dealer."

"Naw, come on? You couldn't have? You would have needed the paperwork for it to do that."

"Yeah, and I had the paperwork."

"Really? How did you?"

"You left it laying on the dresser in the bedroom."

"Man! I was wondering what the hell I did with it."

"Well now you know."

"Yeah okay. Ha, ha, ha, very funny… But even with the paperwork you shouldn't have been able to. So how did you?"

"I told the guy at the store I was your wife."

"Ah, ha ha, ha ha, my wife! Really?"

"Yep."

"Wow, and he obviously fell for it?"

"Yep, he sure did... You're not mad are you? Because as your counselor I was only trying to help you."

"No I'm not mad. In fact I'm actually quite amused, and also glad you did what you did."

"Glad? Really?"

"Yeah, I wanted that damn thing gone anyways. Plus you saved me the trouble of doing it myself... Wait... That was your plan all along. Wasn't it?"

"Maybe?"

"Maybe? Yeah I bet it was."

"Like I said. Maybe?"

Their eyes met again, they both tingled, and Susan felt herself begin to blush.

"You're not going to tell me are you?"

Their eyes went deeper into one another's.

"Nope. Doctor-patient confidentiality prohibits me from saying anything."

"Oh, that's low."

"Maybe?"

Their eye's were now locked into one another's, and their bodies went warm.

"Well you could at least tell me how much you got for it?"

They drew closer to each other.

Susan quivered.

Mark said, "Naw, you know what? I don't care what you got for it. Nor do I want the money, you keep it for your trouble."

Their faces drew closer, and Susan softly asked as she began to tingle from the inside-out with hormonal emotion, "Are you sure?"

Mark lowly replied as he slowly leaned in, "Yes, I'm positive."

One of the movers then stepped into the room and interrupted.

They almost kissed.

"Mark."

"Yeah?" Mark replied as he and Susan were startled away from each other.

She cleared her throat and stared back out the window.

"We're finished."

"Oh, alright. I guess that means you and your crew would like to get paid?"

"Well yeah." The mover replied with a sarcastic laugh, "That would be nice."

Mark chuckled and said as Susan giggled, "Alright, if you insist. Susan I'll be right back."

"Okay…"

She cleared her throat again.

Mark followed the mover outside and jokingly asked, "Cash is okay, isn't it?"

"Yeah if you insist." The mover replied and then laughed.

Mark then pulled a roll of one hundred dollar bills from his pocket, counted out fifteen of them, signed a bill of service, paid the mover, and said, "Keep the change."

The mover gave Mark a receipt, shook his hand, and said, " Okay, thanks, and have a nice day."

"You too." Mark happily replied.

He then went back inside…

Susan and Mark then spent the rest of the day talking, flirting, unpacking Mark's things, and getting it all organized. They took their time at it, and they both enjoyed every single minute of it, and they both enjoyed each other. The day was so nice, and full of positive energy that the two of them wanted it to never end. For the both of them, things just kept getting better and better, they felt great, and the chemicals between them just kept brewing, and brewing. There was definitely a sense of love in the air, and they were starting to become drunk with it; especially Susan. At certain points of the day all she could think about, and badly wanted to do, was jump on Mark, tear all of his clothes off, and forcibly have violent, passionate sex with him. She visualized it, and it burnt her up. Of course she never showed it, she just kept thinking about it, and it almost drove her crazy; she contained herself though.

Other times during the day she thought about what it would be like if Mark just took hold of her, pulled her pants down, and forced himself on her. *Oh! That would be so great*, Susan thought, *if he threw me to the floor, forcibly ripped my pants and underwear off, and pounded me from behind against my ass as hard as he could while I screamed the whole time. Aw! And after he was done, mm, he would drag me into the bedroom by my hair and force me to play with myself while he watched. MM, and God his dick looks so big. I'd just love right now to wrap my lips around it. Keep dreaming, Susan. Hmm maybe someday? Mm, God I hope so!*

She definitely had it bad for him…

Later that evening they went to dinner at a very nice restaurant, and while eating, Susan confessed a secret to Mark; she felt he deserved to know the truth about what had really happened to her. She was also still having very erotic thoughts about him, and was now madly in love him; so much that it was burning her up. She just wasn't to sure if Mark had any deep feelings for her, so for now, she decided to keep that part to herself. From the very beginning she had always sort of had a thing for him, it was just now even more so, and Kara's comment to Mark at the gateway center was certainly right.

Maybe all along that was the cause of Susan's Stomachaches?

"Mark, I have a confession to make."

Chewing up the food he had in his mouth, and swallowing it, Mark then asked, "Really, what kind of confession?"

"Well first you have to promise you won't get mad."

"Okay." Mark replied and kept eating.

So did Susan.

"I really wasn't in a car accident."

"Okay…" Mark said, then asked as he kept eating, "Then what happened?"

"I had a breakdown."

"Really?"

"Yeah, and from what I've gathered, it was a bad one."

"From what you've gathered, what's that mean?"

"It means I don't really remember any of it."

"Wow. That's not good."

"Well no, not really. In a way, not remembering is kind of a good thing."

"Yeah, I guess it sort of would be."

"You're not mad are you?"

"No, just a little confused."

"Confused?"

"Yeah, confused as to why you just didn't tell me, and well. Hmm, maybe I should say, curious?"

"Curious?"

"Yeah, curious as to what happened and why?"

"Well what we think happened."

"We?"

"Yes we. The prestigious psychologist has momentarily became the nut, and has had to seek professional help herself."

Mark laughed at what Susan said, and momentarily choked on his food in the process. The way she said what she had said struck him so funny that he couldn't help but laugh.

Susan laughed as well, and asked, "Pretty funny huh?"

"No not really. Just the way you put it is what made it funny."

They both laughed again…

Mark asked with concern, "So what happened?"

"Well my Doctor says, because of the stress from my husbands death, and going back to work to soon, that I probably didn't mourn long enough, and it caused me to have a subconscious breakdown that took over my mind and became conscious."

"Really, do you think he's right?"

"Unfortunately, yeah I do. But don't worry, I won't go psycho on you. The short-term meds that I'm now on will prevent it from happening again."

Mark chewed some food, swallowed it, and laughed, "Psycho huh?"

Susan forked some food to her mouth, chewed it up, swallowed it, and laughed as well, "Yeah, psycho. I mean I don't wanna scare you off, that's just the simplest way to put it."

"Oh no, you're not gonna scare me off. Nope; not gonna happen."

"Good, but I guess I really went totally nuts. Of course I don't remember any of it."

"Nothing?"

"Nope. Nothing."

"Wow."

Mark kept eating.

"All I remember is waking up stitched up, bandaged up, feeling extremely drugged, sore, and strapped to a hospital bed."

"That had to have been frightening."

Susan ate, and said, "It was. But what was more frightening than that, to me anyways, was that my sister had found me lying on the floor naked surrounded by a smashed up mirror, and when I woke up for a moment in the ambulance, I had went so crazy that the E.M.Ts had to sedate me by force."

"Wow. Yeah, that would be frightening. You're doing alright now, right?"

"Yes, I'm doing fine. Gonna be on the meds for a while though. Oh, and please, please don't think that you're hanging around with some loony ass bitch, because it's really not like that."

Laughing for a moment, Mark said as Susan laughed as well, "I don't think that at all."

"Good."

Susan felt really warm on the inside, and Mark really liked her sense of humor, in a way it sort of reminded him of Kara's; she sometimes spoke the same way.

Susan ate some more, then asked as Mark ate as well, "So again, you're not mad at me are you? Because I really wanted to tell you before, I just felt stupid, and plus I didn't wanna scare you off."

Mark swallowed, and replied, "No I'm not mad at all. I totally understand."

"Good."

They continued to eat…

Hearing that Mark wasn't mad made Susan feel even warmer on the inside. She also tingled, and wanted so badly to sleep with him, that it made her inner thighs quiver, but she knew that it was probably to soon, so she kept that to herself. For a short second again, she even momentarily visualized them being together and began to blush. But as soon as the vision came, it went, and Mark didn't even notice.

He said, "I probably would have done the same thing, but, just for future reference, seeing how I'm the one that tried to kill himself, and I should have scared you off, don't be afraid to tell me anything, and never feel stupid about it."

Susan's body then flooded with loving hormones from Mark's comments, her thighs throbbed even harder, and her labia began to swell open.

Trying to shake the feeling off, she kept eating, laughed, then replied, "Okay Doctor Mark."

Mark laughed as well, and kept eating.

They were falling in love, and now that Mark was healed, he in a way was helping Susan heal. It was as if they had needed each other, and the cosmic forces that controlled the universe had brought them together.

Mark had, had his time, and now it was hers.

35

Friday evening, after they finished with dinner, Mark and Susan did some grocery shopping, and went back to the cottage. Talking for a while, and watching a couple of DVDS, they soon found themselves feeling tired and wanting to go to sleep. Naturally, after he insisted, Mark slept in the living room recliner he had usually slept in, and Susan got the bed in the bedroom. She would have gladly slept in the recliner, but Mark refused to let her. She would have also gladly shared the bed and herself with Mark that night. In fact she had actually hoped for it; the thought of it made her tingle all over. But that didn't happen, it was to soon, and deep down inside she knew it was, and it was okay. Because she was having such a wonderful time, it was nice just being there with him; that's what really mattered. *But hey,* Susan thought as she laid down and drifted off to sleep, *I can always wish... Hmm, maybe someday?*

Mark didn't feel the same way though. Yes he was enjoying himself, yes he was enjoying her company, and yes he was falling for her. But the thought of sharing the bed and himself with her didn't even cross his mind. For the moment, all he thought about until he fell asleep, was how wonderful it was to be at the cottage. It was always one of the only places he had ever been that had truly felt like home to him, and how nice it was to be sharing it with someone whom he considered to be a friend. It was all so wonderful, Mark felt bliss. It also felt good to him to not feel alone anymore. For the first time, in a long,

long time, everything felt truly peaceful, and he felt whole again. Mark never wanted to leave this place, and unless it was for business, he never would again. Sometimes for some of us, dreams do truly come true, and for Mark, part of his was…

He slept that night with a very warm heart…

36

The next morning while Susan was sleeping, Mark woke up really early, used the bathroom, and made the both of them breakfast. Shortly before he finished, Susan woke up and joined him. They sat together in the cottage's beach side screen porch, and casually talked and ate while the warm sun slowly came up. Afterwards they both got ready for the day. Naturally Mark insisted on Susan showering first, which she did, and naturally she would have shared the shower with him, and even though she wanted so, so badly to suggest it to him, she didn't. She knew it was still to soon for something like that, and she was okay with it. But still, just the thought of it made her insides throb in ways that she had never thought possible. She was experiencing feelings that she had never felt before. Not even for her deceased husband, and she really loved him, and she always would. But the love and yearning she was feeling for Mark was different. Different in ways that she would never be able to explain. Why? She didn't know. And why? She really didn't care. For her it was way to wonderful of a feeling to try and figure it all out. She just hoped it would stay that way, and that it wasn't just some kind of crazy crush that would fade with time. Plus all she really knew was the more time she had spent with Mark, the deeper her feelings became, and it looked to her as if it was all met to be.

For Mark it was something that he had wanted to take his time with, and yes, he was developing deep feelings for her. But, he felt that even though she had been his doctor for a short while, he still didn't really know much about her. But yet, he had a strong, strong feeling that he was going to learn a lot more, and things with them were going to go much, much further; and that was just fine with him. In fact, it was more than fine with him. It was exactly what he had wanted.

While Susan was showering, Mark went into the bedroom and finished packing up Kara's things. Everything was almost as he had left it when he was there before, which was cool for him because he thought, *Well that's less work I'll have to do. Better finish before Susan gets out though. Ha, ha, ha. The way she's been looking at me I might get fucking raped. That wasn't nice Mark. Yeah? Maybe? Hee, hee, hee, it might not be a bad idea either. Shut up Mark! Can't rape the willing! Yeah, and right now I'm not willing. Liar! Maybe?*

Mark kept packing, and one of the boxes that he filled with some of Kara's stuff he set aside to send to her mom and dad; later he would take it to the post office. The others that were filled with clothes, shoes, and other things, would go to a donation center.

When Mark finished, he took all the boxes outside and carefully packed them into his car. After he was done, he looked at his other car; the one that sat for the winter, and said to himself, "I think maybe I should start that thing."

He went back inside, fetched his keys, went back outside, and to his surprise, when he went to start the car, it fired right up. "Wow! I must have gotten lucky." Mark said to himself, "I thought for sure the battery would be dead."

He then got out of the car, and let it run while he went back inside for a minute.

Susan was also done with the bathroom, "It's all yours," she said as she came out in a bath towel, and brushed against him while she passed by on her way to the bedroom.

She did it on purpose.

Mark didn't mind though, he hadn't felt the softness of a woman's body in so long that he got a quick rock-hard boner from her touch, and he just replied in a funny fashion, "Oh, alright."

He quickly shook off what had just happened, and asked Susan through the bedroom door, "In about ten minutes, if I'm not out, will you go and shut my other car off?"

"Sure."

"K, thanks."

Mark then went into the bathroom, closed the door behind him, got ready for his shower, and thought, Whew! I should make this a cold one. Hmm, crazy-woman. I know she did that on purpose. Luckily for me, I'm a gentleman… I think?

After his shower Mark got himself ready to go.

He and Susan took a ride into the city, and dropped the boxes of Kara's things off at a secondhand store. They then dropped off the ones set aside for her parents at a post office. After that for a few hours they went driving around sight-seeing.

Afterwards they stopped at a pizza place for lunch, and then went back to the cottage. They were both having such a wonderful time, that time itself didn't seem to matter. In fact they lost all track of it, and soon after long walks on the beach, hiking, bicycling through wooded trails, and a nightly bonfire, plus some wonderfully prepared and shared meals, the weekend was over; it flew by, and it, for the both of them all went to fast.

Because of Susan's Doctor's appointments, she had to leave

Monday morning. Mark tried insisting on driving her home; she wouldn't have it. So Mark tried insisting that she take one of his cars. She wouldn't have it; she felt Mark had already done enough. Plus she had to be back really early, which meant leaving really early, and she didn't want to put that on Mark either. He didn't care though, but she still refused. She did agree on flying home though. She just wouldn't let Mark pay the charter service bill. She paid it, and early Monday morning Mark drove her to the county's airport, and dropped her off at the charter service's hanger.

He walked her to the door, and they stopped before she went inside.

Susan turned to Mark and looked deep into his eyes.

He said, "Well, I had a wonderful time."

Susan's insides throbbed, and she replied, "So did I."

She put her right hand softly on Mark's right cheek and continued, "In fact it was more than wonderful."

Mark took a deep breath and asked, "Maybe we can do it again sometime?"

"I hope so." Susan whispered as she leaned in, softly kissed him on the cheek, and gently hugged him, "I sure hope so."

She then stepped back and said as she looked into Mark's eye's with a loving lustful look, "I'll be seeing you."

"Call me when you get in."

"I will."

Susan smiled and rubbed Mark's face again. She wanted to deeply kiss him, so, badly, that it was burning her up, and melting her insides. But, she didn't. *It's to soon,* She thought. So she just softly said, "Bye," and then turned around and walked away.

She didn't want to leave, and Mark really didn't want her to…

37

About an hour and a half after her plane took off, it arrived and landed at Susan's hometown airport. Shortly after, she caught a cab ride home.

When she got home, and after she paid her cab fare, Susan gathered her things together, went inside, and immediately called Mark.

The call rang, and went through. Mark answered, "Hey! I see you made it home okay."

"I sure did."

"Good, I'm glad to hear it."

"Can't talk long though, have to get ready for my appointment. Can I call you again when I get back? There's something I wanna talk to you about."

"Um yeah, sure. But can you?"

"Okay smart-ass."

Mark started laughing.

Susan responded to him with sarcasm, "May! I call you later? Fucker…"

Mark laughed harder and replied "Fucker? Yes you may."

They both then laughed simultaneously, and Susan said, "Bye, Fucker."

Mark laughed even harder, and said, "Bye, talk to you later." He ended the call laughing.

Susan put her phone down, giggled, and went into the bathroom to freshen up. When she was finished, she left her house and drove to her doctor's appointment.

After the appointment, she went back home, went in, used the bathroom, and got herself something to eat.

When she was finished, she called Mark again. The call rang through, Mark answered, "Hey, this is Fucker."

Susan laughed and replied, "Hey."

The sound of his voice made her tingle.

"So how was your appointment?"

"It was okay."

"Just okay?"

"Well yeah, it was just a typical visit. You know, a lot of questions, and a lot of answers."

"Yeah good point. So how are you doing? You know, with what had happened?"

"I'm doing great, in fact, I'm feeling wonderful. The doctor thinks the time I spent there with you did me a lot of good. And he said if I feel like I'm ready, that I can return to work."

"Really? Wow, that's great!"

"Isn't it though?"

"So are you going back anytime soon?"

"Hmm…"

"Susan?"

"Well, that's what I wanted to talk to you about. That's if you wanna hear it?"

"Yeah, shoot."

"Well I… Hmm… After I get rid of this house and mostly everything that's in it. I was thinking about leaving my practice, of course I would turn it over to my partner after she found an intern."

"Okay."

"I would then find an apartment up by you, and start

another practice someplace in Alpena. What do you think?"

Mark's heart skipped a beat from what Susan had just said, and he tingled from head to toe with excitement, but he didn't let Susan know it. He kept his cool and replied "Yeah, that sounds great. Well, except for one part."

"What part's that?"

"The part about you getting an apartment, I won't have it."

"What do you mean?"

"I mean you can stay with me. Well that's if you want to?"

Susan's heart melted.

"You mean live together?"

"Yeah for a while. Hell, I'll even let you have the bedroom. That's if you'd like?"

"Sure Mark, I'd love to. But you know, you don't have to?"

"Yeah, but I want to."

Susan tingled even more, and said, "Okay then. I'll start getting things ready here, and I'll keep you informed on what's going on."

"Okay. Um, do you still have the number that I gave you for the home donation center?"

"Yep, I sure do."

"All righty then. Now when would you like me to come down and lend you a hand? I'm leaving for my book tour in two weeks, and I won't be able to help then. But in the meantime, I really don't have much of anything to do."

Even though Susan wanted badly for Mark to come down, she refused his help, and said, "Oh no, you're not doing any more for me. You've already done enough."

"Oh come on, I could."

Susan kindly cut him off.

"No Mark, I'll manage. Besides, my sister lives close by and I'm sure she'll be more than willing to help me out. Plus, I'm just gonna do what you did."

"What's that? Hire a crew?"

"Yep, you got it."

Mark laughed, "I don't blame you." He then asked, "Because of your practice and everything, it's probably gonna take longer than two weeks for you to close it all up you think?"

"Yeah more than likely. Why?"

"Well I'd like to be here when you get here, but I guess that's not gonna happen."

"No, probably not."

"Okay then, I tell you what. I just got an email from Andrea with my tour schedule. I'm multitasking right now. Anyways, it looks like I've got the first two weeks of June off. So, how about we try and plan something nice for then?"

"Sounds good, and I'll be keeping in touch."

"Okay great, bye."

"Alright bye. Oh, and Mark?"

"Yeah?"

"Thanks again."

"You bet, and I'll be seeing you."

"You can count on it."

Susan ended the call, tossed her phone down while she did a crazy happy dance, and yelled, "Whew!"

She ran into her bedroom, jumped up from the floor onto her bed, wildly hopped up and down on it like a happy little girl, and kept yelling, "Whew! Yes! I can't believe it! I'm so fucking happy! Whew!"

After a moment, when she realized she wasn't quite acting

her age, she stopped hopping, kicked her shoes off in the process, landed on the bed butt first, and sort of felt stupid.

She thought, Woman, how old are you? You're acting like a five-year-old. Ah, who cares, it's not like any one saw me or heard me.

Laying down and hugging a pillow, She said to herself, "Whew, now I think it's time for a nap."

Two and a half weeks later she was living at the cottage and beginning her search for a place to start her new practice. The whole time, on and off, she and Mark kept in touch with each other, and she was also now totally in love with him. All she wanted was him, and when he came back from his tour, she planned on telling him exactly how she felt; she just hoped that he felt the same way.

38

Soon before Susan and Mark knew it, it was June first. The weather was warm, the sky was a clear deep dark blue, the beach around the bay was a beautiful light golden brown color, the lake water had a warm magnificent-looking blue and greenish hue to it, and it looked as smooth as perfectly polished glass. The air smelled of fresh pine, and was also mixed in with the light scent of bonfire smoke from the camper's nightly fires in the local campground; it was all so truly amazing, and completely intoxicating.

Mark was supposed to be back then, but he wasn't. There were some things that his publisher wanted him to do. So it would be another few days before he could come home, which sort of bummed Susan and Mark out. Especially Susan; she was looking so forward to seeing him that it was burning her up. She yearned to see him so bad, that at times for reasons she didn't understand, it almost drove her nuts. She controlled it though. By occupying herself with plenty of things to do, and also spending a lot of time getting her new practice up and running, she literally stopped herself from going crazy again. And soon the extra few days went by, and Mark came home.

The day his plane was due to arrive was a beautiful warm summer day in Northern Michigan. The humidity was low, a light breeze bristled through the trees and grass, the sky was a deep beautiful blue, a few snowy white clouds hung in the air, the waters of Lake Huron were calm and crystal clear, the air again, all around, smelled fresh, and was again filled with the wonderful aroma of pine and smoke. In a sense, it was heavenly, and very peaceful.

For Susan it was all just so amazing. She had never, except for the time she and her sister had stayed the week there, experienced, or ever felt the kind of energy that she was feeling. It was all such an emotional wonderful high for her that she never wanted to come down. She was so warm with emotion, that in a way she was drunk with it. For her, it was truly an amazing feeling, the bruise on her face was gone, her hands were no longer stitched and bandaged, and even though they would always bear the scars of her breakdown, Susan had decided that she would never look back again; she was healed. Plus the excitement she was feeling because she was going to get to see Mark, and finally get to spend some time with him was almost overwhelming, so much as that, that it totally over-road anything that could have caused her to have a relapse. She was even off from her meds. She felt great, and she had never before felt the way she was feeling in her whole life, about anyone or anything. Why? She didn't know. She just did, and she just went with it.

When Susan got herself ready to go and pick Mark up from the Airport, she dolled herself up and made herself look nice. Not to nice though, she didn't want Mark to think that she was trying to impress him; so she slightly toned it down. Not to much though, she also didn't want to look like a pig, so she kept herself at a happy medium; which she was satisfied with.

She was so, so happy, she couldn't wait. She was also slightly nervous as well, she had no clue as to how things were going to go. She decided rather than anticipate anything, she would just wing it.

When she left, Susan sort of hurried and arrived at the Airport an hour early. That was okay with her though, she had no problem with waiting. She'd been waiting for over a month to see Mark, *So what was another hour,* Susan thought as she parked her car, went inside, and patiently waited.

Soon the hour went by, and a terminal board lit up with the arrival of a flight; it was Mark's.

Susan's heart skipped a beat, and she also got Goosebumps.

Shortly after, Mark walked into the building pulling his wheeled luggage behind him.

Susan spotted him right away, and her stomach did a flip.

She shook for a moment, and her heart pounded.

She swallowed, and took a deep breath as she went to meet him.

Mark looked so, so handsome and masculine to her, that she wanted badly to run up and start hugging and kissing him, but she didn't; she contained herself. Instead, she stepped to him and said while she softly touched his face, passionately looked into his eyes, and smiled, "Hey handsome. How are you?"

"Good." Mark replied and said, "You look nice."

"Well thank you." Susan happily replied.

They hugged…

Susan also kissed Mark's cheek and said, "It's nice to see you." She also asked as she stepped back, "Are you hungry?"

"Yeah, as a matter of fact, I'm starving."

"Okay lets go then, and I'm doing the cooking when we get home."

"You know you don't have to?"

"Yeah I know, but I want to."

"Okay." Mark replied, and then asked as they made their

way out of the building and to the car, "What'cha gonna make?"

"Well I was thinking about a spaghetti with meat sauce. Some cheesy garlic bread, and a nice red Merlot to wash it down with. How's that sound?"

"Sounds great." Mark replied as they got into the car, "In fact, I'm so hungry and it sounds so good, I think I can already taste it."

Mark's comment made Susan laugh.

Mark laughed as well.

She then started the car and drove home. They made small talk as they went, and she tingled the whole time. She was on cloud nine, and sometime after they ate, she was going to tell Mark exactly how she felt; she had to. She just hoped that he had felt the same way, which to her surprise, after they ate and took a long walk on the beach along the shore; she found out that he did.

She became so warm with emotion when she found out how he felt that it almost made her cry. She didn't tell him, he told her first. In fact after their walk, Mark started a small bonfire at sunset, sat Susan down in a chair by the fire, fetched a large blanket from inside, got down on the ground on his knees in front of her, pulled a gold ring with a huge diamond on it from his pocket, and calmly said as he took her by the hand, "I already called your dad and asked if this was okay, and he said yes. So will you marry me?"

Susan sat in shock for a moment, filled with burning warmth, accepted the ring, and put it on while she tried not to cry. She couldn't believe what was happening.

She trembled for a moment, looked Mark in the eye and

said, "Yes, I'll marry you."

Mark melted.

"But you have to tell me one thing?"

"What's that?"

Susan laughed and asked, "How and the hell did you get my dads' number?"

"I went through your phone the weekend you stayed with me."

"You sneaky brat."

"You're not mad are you?"

"No, not at all." Susan replied with a laugh, "It's actually funny, and very sweet at the same time."

She leaned to Mark, kissed him, and continued as her body burned, and her inner thighs painfully throbbed, "I love you, and I've loved you for quite some time, and I would be honored to be your wife."

They kissed again, which quickly turned into a very deep, passionate, and long lasting kiss.

Stopping for a moment, the two of them looked deep into one another's eyes while Susan grabbed the blanket, kissed Mark again, and undressed as they wrapped the blanket around one another. As nighttime came, and their fire slightly died down, they fell to the sandy ground, and made hard, passionate love. Under the star-filled sky, Mark and Susan's souls and bodies, in a heavy, emotional, and somewhat violent display of Mother Nature's ballet of exotic love and sensuous expression, became one.

Their pulses raced, their organs throbbed, their bodies burned, he went into her, and with every powerful thrust, with every deep kiss, they became more and more entranced.

Time seemed to stand still…

She moaned, he moaned, her breasts swelled, he went deeper, she cried harder, he pounded, her labia and vulva suctioned loudly, and grew wider, and wider, their skin slapped loudly, her button became harder and harder, he became harder and harder.

She was drenched. He was drenched.

He moaned. She moaned and convulsed.

He convulsed. She orgasmed .

Mark came powerfully, and deeply within her.

They were soaked in deep passion. The both of them were entranced, and in a totally different state of being.

Six more times she came. Six more times he came.

Hours went by without notice.

Then exhaustion set in, and they collapsed into each other's arms.

Panting wildly, and gasping for air, they soon fell asleep without a word, and woke the next day at sunrise. Face to face, as a warm breeze blew across the land, the forest, the water, the sand, their hair and face, without saying a word, they woke up and just stared into one another's eyes. For the both of them, it was as if time had stood still, and they were in a dream. A deep, deep dream that the two of them didn't ever want to wake from.

39

Soon before Mark and Susan knew it, Mark's two weeks off were over, then June was over, and it was July, which meant that Mark's book tour was over, and he would be coming home. It also meant he was going to be able to spend some more quality time with Susan, and that was something he was really looking forward to. It seemed to him that no matter how much time they had together, that it was never enough, and the whole time Mark was gone; that's all he could think about. He wanted to spend every spare moment that he had with her. In fact, Mark couldn't get enough of Susan, and Susan couldn't get enough of him. For the two of them, it was a constant twenty four hour love buzz; one that just wouldn't quit. And as soon as Susan picked Mark up on July first from the Airport, and they got home, they immediately had a repeat of what had happened the night Mark had asked her to marry him; except this time it took place inside.

The next morning it happened again.

Afterwards Mark's phone rang. Susan was fast asleep, and he really didn't want to answer it. But he also didn't want the ringing to disturb her. So he fumbled around the room for a minute trying to find it, and when he finally did, he answered it.

"Hello."

"Mark?"

"Yeah Andrea it's me. What's up?"

"Well I know it's early, and you just got back yesterday, and I'm sorry to be bothering you this soon. But this is really important… Mark, are you there?"

"Yeah I'm here. So what's up, what's so important?"

"Well a few things."

"Okay?"

"Well first, your recent work just went all the way to number one. My congrats."

"Thank you."

"And the concepts you wrote about on health care made an impression on the president."

"The president? You mean the president, as the president of the United States, or the president of the company?"

"Your first choice would be the one."

"Really, how did he? You know what, never mind, I don't wanna know."

"Are you sure?"

"Yeah, I'm positive."

"Somehow I knew you were gonna say that."

"Yeah well, you know me. Mr. Doesn't Like To Know Much."

"Oh whatever Mark."

"Ah, ha ha ha, well it's true."

"Yeah right. Anyways, two days after the fourth, which would be Monday the sixth. Some place in New York City, we're not sure of the venue yet, I'll email you all the info later when we know."

"Oh, okay."

"Are you ready?"

"Yeah sure, shoot, I'm all ears."

"There's gonna be a banquet and a ball held in your honor, and the president himself has requested that he be there to meet you, and he also wants to give a speech about the content of your book, which I noticed was inspired by your now fiancee?"

"Yep, that's correct. If it wasn't for her being in my life, and inspiring me, I never would have written it."

"Aw… That's so sweet. You know she's invited as well."

"Yeah, I kind of figured that."

"What's her name again?"

"Susan."

"Well you tell Susan that I said congrats on the engagement."

"Oh I sure will."

"Good, and I'm looking forward to seeing you both on the sixth. That's if you're gonna go…"

"Well yeah."

"And Susan?"

"Yeah, I don't see why not. I mean she's started a new practice here, but it doesn't officially open for another three weeks."

"Well good, that's great! I'm happy to hear it!"

"Yeah me too."

"Okay, well then I guess I'll be seeing you, and I'll email you the rest of the details later. Sound good to you?"

"Yeah, sounds great."

"Okay… Whoa wait! One more thing. When's the wedding?"

"We haven't set a date yet, and all we know is it's gonna be sometime next spring. We wanna take our time. If, you know what I mean?"

"Oh yeah, I definitely know what you mean."

"Yeah, I thought you would."

"Okay then, I guess we're all set, and I'll be speaking with you soon."

"You bet."

"Alright, bye for now."

"Bye."

Mark then hit the hang up button on his phone and tossed it to the floor.

He then curled up against Susan's backside, played with her butt for a minute, then fell asleep.

A few hours later they both woke up and had sex again.

Afterwards, they both laid for a while, and Mark told Susan about the phone call he had gotten from Andrea, and what was gonna happen on the sixth. She became so excited from the news that her whole body tingled with warm emotion; she couldn't believe it, she was so excited for him and herself, she also couldn't help but think, *Only a short while ago I had gone through what some would consider to be a virtual hell, and now the man that I'm going to marry is going to be met by the president.* She was so proud of him, and so happy that she was going to be there to share it all with him. It was all so wonderful, and she felt wonderful.

Mark didn't really care though, for him it was just going to be another ceremony. Of course he didn't tell Susan that; he didn't want to spoil her mood. Seeing her that happy made him happy, and really at the time, to Mark that's all that mattered. No one knew it yet, but Mark was gonna be done with books. He had other plans, and he had plenty of money and time to follow through with them. He just had to wait for the right time to tell everyone, and now definitely wasn't the right time. Susan was so happy, and so was the publishing company. In all reality though, Mark knew deep down inside that if his books weren't doing as well as they were, that the company wouldn't be kissing his ass the way they'd been kissing it, and that had always somewhat annoyed him. At times it even troubled him, but he didn't let it show, and he wouldn't let it show. Because when things started going good for him; "good," meaning his rise in the book industry, he made an inner pact with himself never to take any of it too seriously. Never let it go to his head, always smile and accept what was given to him, never turn away money, and never get your hopes up. Don't attach yourself to business partners, or to anyone that he felt was gonna hold him down. Never by any means respect anyone that doesn't respect him, and live to the fullest. Because this life was the only one he had to live. Plus, if you have to fake your way through some situations, then fake it; no one will ever know the difference, and that's what he intended on doing at the banquet dinner. He would just fake his way through, because he honestly didn't care about it. Nor did he really care about meeting the president. *Whoopty-Fucking-Doo!* Mark thought as they got out of bed and Susan happily carried on about the whole thing. She was acting like an excited little girl, and Mark wasn't going to ruin it for her. He'd wait until after the banquet. *Actually,* he thought while they then got ready for the day, *I'm gonna wait for quite a while after. Maybe a month or so? Hmm, the way she's carrying on, I might possibly even wait longer then that? Hmm, we'll see.*

    The rest of the day, and the next few, were spent setting up Susan's new office, and as always, time flew by, and before they knew it, it was time to fly to New York City, which they both really enjoyed. What they enjoyed the most was that they were doing it together; as they always did.

    Shortly after they arrived, they took a cab to a beautiful

high-rise hotel that was like a miniature city in itself, and checked in.

Their suite was on the twenty-first floor, and every large room, including the bathroom, had a breath-taking view of the city. The room was rather exquisite, which was a little to much for Mark's taste, but it made Susan happy and she loved it. So Mark just went with it.

After they got settled in, they rested for a while, and then went and ate at one of the hotel's many restaurants.

They also met up with Mark's rep, Andrea. She sat and ate with them while she updated Mark with some last-minute details.

The banquet would take place the following evening in a large hall in the same building. Susan couldn't wait, she tingled from head to toe with excitement.

Mark just couldn't wait to get it over with and get back home. He planned on starting his flying lessons when they got back, and Susan's new practice would be up and running; so they were going to be busy.

40

The day of the banquet was a busy day for everyone involved, it was especially busy for all of the hotel workers and the publishing company's employees. Everywhere one looked, there were people bustling about and getting done what needed to be done to make the coming event happen. Because of the president's later appearance, the whole place was also a fortress, and had been a for quite some time. There were Secret Service people everywhere, and security was very, very tight. For Mark and Susan though, it was pretty laid back. They just basically hung out in their room and enjoyed each other's company. They talked a lot, and they also did a lot of what most new couples do at the start of a heated relationship; which was perfectly fine with them. If it would have been up to Mark, that's all that they would have done, but he knew that wouldn't be possible; so he carried on regardless.

That evening everything at the banquet went pretty much as planned, and as Mark had expected, people talked, they drank, they shook hands, Mark made a speech, other authors made speeches, a few other people made one, and the president spoke; which to Mark, was nothing new.

Mark and Susan, plus many others, including the C.E.O of Mark's publishing company were also personally introduced to the president, and over dinner Mark actually spent a good forty-five minutes talking with him, which Mark thought was sort of cool, but not really, he was more interested in Susan. He couldn't believe how totally ravishing she looked in the black dress and silver jewelry she had on. He just couldn't keep his eyes off her, nor could she keep her eyes off him. If it had been up to the both of them, especially Mark, they would have been someplace else, doing something else. The chemicals between them were just so intoxicating, that they were both painfully drunk in love with each other, and everyone around them could tell, because they just totally glowed from it.

Soon after everyone finished eating, some local DJ said a few things, then the music started, the drinks began to flow, and people started to dance.

Susan, while Mark was talking with a few people who had sat with him, excused herself for a moment. She told Mark she'd be right back.

Mark kissed her and said, "Alright, just make sure you hurry back."

Susan whispered back in his ear as she lightly bit it, "Oh don't worry, I will." She then turned and walked away, and Mark went back to his conversation.

Fifteen minutes later Mark's phone vibrated in his pocket.

He pulled it out and checked it.

It was a text from Susan that said, My stomach's upset for some reason. Went to our room to lay down for a while. Love you, have fun, and I'll wait up for you.

Mark replied back, Okay, well I hope you feel better. Love you too, and I won't be long.

A half an hour later Mark snuck out, and went to check on Susan.

When he got to their room, he opened the door, stepped inside, closed the door behind him, called Susan's name, and then stood frozen in total, complete shock at what he was seeing; Mark just couldn't believe his eyes.

His assistant and also publicist Andrea, sat across the room. She was beaten, gagged, tied to a chair, crying, and trying to break free.

Susan then stepped into the room from the bedroom while Mark remained frozen.

She had a gun. It was the same gun that Mark had used when he tried to kill himself. How she got it into the building, Mark had no clue?

She was also dressed in Kara's purple gown. The gown that Mark had set aside and had obviously forgotten about.

Her hair and makeup were also done up like Kara's, and she had a completely different look in her eyes. A look that Mark had never seen before.

She looked as though she had totally checked out of reality.

Mark couldn't believe it. He was stunned; he was confused, and Susan quickly pointed the gun at Andrea's head.

Andrea squirmed.

Susan's hand's shook.

Mark slowly asked, "Susan, what's going on?"

Susan started crying, then frantically screamed while her tears flowed, "She can't have you!"

She also moved the gun closer to Andrea's head and yelled while Andrea began to cry.

"Shut up! Shut the Fuck up!"

Mark looked at them both and calmly responded, "Whoa Susan, calm down, and tell me what you're talking about."

Susan yelled, "I said she can't have you! No one can!"

Andrea stopped crying and just quivered.

Susan cried, "I know she wants you, and fuck you! You want

her too!"

Mark slowly stepped to Susan.

She pointed the gun at him and cried, "You did! Didn't you Mark! I bet you did!"

"What are you talking about?"

"You know what I'm talking about! You fucked her didn't you! Already! You already fucked her!

"Susan, I don't know what?"

"Yeah you did! You fucked her already! A lot sooner then you fucked me!"

Susan cried harder.

Mark stepped closer and said, "Look! I don't know what you're talking about, or what's going on. But you need to put the gun down, calm down, and we'll talk this through."

"No! Fuck you!" Susan screamed, then cried, "Why Mark? Why? I loved you from the get go! How could you?"

"Susan. I haven't done anything, I…"

"Shut up! Just to think, I killed my husband to be with you!"

"You did what?"

"Yep, I sure did. I also killed that fucking stupid wife of yours!"

Mark's heart sank.

He stepped closer and said, "You killed… You killed Kara?" He could hardly get the question out, "How? Why?"

Susan shook and said, "I followed her to her goddamn favorite coffee shop. The stupid bitch didn't even know I was there."

"You…" Mark tried to say.

His mind flashed to a visual of the whole thing while Susan kept talking.

"And I drugged her coffee while she had her back turned."

"How! Did, why?"

"I'm a Doctor, Mark. I knew the drug I gave her would never come up in a test."

"Why... You. But!" Mark stepped closer, and he just couldn't get his words out.

Susan continued as Mark's mind flashed again, "The stupid bitch's heart probably stopped while she was driving!"

Mark suddenly felt sick as he asked, "Your husband, you did the same thing to him?"

"What do you think Mark!? You're not fucking stupid are you!?"

Susan then pointed the gun back at Andrea's head and said, "Oh, and unlike you, I remembered the fucking bullets!"

Mark shivered and asked as he shook the vision from his head, "You planned the whole thing, why Susan, why did you?"

Susan cried, "Because I had to have you! I love you, and I wanted you from the very beginning, and there was no other way." Susan's tone then changed to one of deep anger while she said, "But now, this, this fucking cunt had to come along and ruin the whole thing."

"It's not like that."

"Yes it is Mark! And you fucking know it!"

"No it's not."

Mark stepped closer while Susan shook. He immediately realized that the gun was the one that she had claimed to have gotten rid of for him, he said, "Susan don't do this. Lets just end it and we'll talk about it."

"I'm gonna end it now!" Susan screamed.

Andrea cried. Then in a single instance, the past three years of Mark's life flashed before his eyes. He felt anger, he felt dirty, he felt used, he felt disgusted, and he quickly lunged at Susan as she went to pull the trigger.

Susan immediately fell backwards, the gun fired, the bullet hit the ceiling, Susan tripped over her own feet, and instantly flew through a window screaming and firing the gun as she fell to the street below and met her death.

The room went silent, and Mark looked out the window…

Staring down at the street below and gazing at Susan's broken, lifeless body as a crowd began to gather around it, Mark stood in shock over what had just happened. He couldn't believe it; it happened so fast. *Wow, I can't believe this shit!* He thought, *I'm never gonna see a shrink again!*

Mark's heart pounding, he rushed to Andrea, quickly untied her, and she jumped into his arms crying.

The standoff was over, and the both of them just stood holding each other in shock until the hotel's security came and kicked the door open.

Two weeks later, after a full legal investigation was done, it was deemed that Mark had acted in the defense of himself and Andrea. He was never arrested, and no charges were ever filed.

Two years later, Mark and Andrea, with the support of family, friends, loved ones, and each other, had gotten over what happened, fell in love with each other, and eventually got married.

One year later Andrea bore Mark the little girl that he had always wanted. They named her Kara Rose, and she looked just like Andrea. She had the prettiest brown hair, the cutest little dimples, and the deepest coal-black, puppy dog eyes that one could ever see; she like her mother was definitely a little heart stealer.

Shortly after, Andrea became pregnant with their second child. This one turned out to be a boy, which they both had also wanted. They named him Jeremy Michael, and he looked just like Mark; he also like his sister was a cute little heart stealer.

Mark, like he had planned, stopped writing books and learned how to fly. He then bought into a Northern Charter Flight Service, which he and Andrea to this day still partially own and operate.

Because of the new additions to the family, the cottage had to be renovated and added onto, which was perfectly fine with the both of them, especially with Mark. He loved his new wife, his new life, and his new family, and he had no plans of ever leaving the cottage or Northern Michigan. He would stay there until the end of his days. He was finally truly happy, and he finally felt complete. So in the end, for the second time in his life, in a roundabout and rather twisted way, Mark had finally gotten a new beginning, and the life he had always dreamed of. His first new beginning was when he was very, very young. In fact he was so young that he doesn't even remember, but the story is this, and one that he swore to his mother and family that would never be told to anyone, and is also all true. Mark, his mother, his dad, his mother's mother, and a few of Mark's aunts and uncles, all traveled to Earth from a distant planet when he was very young. They left their world to escape a violent religious based war his people had been fighting for centuries, and now live here on Earth, in peace and in total secrecy. No one knows about them, not Mark's new wife, not his kids, neither did Kara, and not even the people they had left behind on their home world. They did it all in secrecy, and they destroyed their ship shortly after they arrived; Mark's uncle John was the one that built it and navigated it to Earth.

Sometimes late at night when the stars are out, and no one's around, Mark gazes up at the sky and wonders if there is anyone else left; he also wonders what his home planet might look like. The stories he's been told by his mother really don't do his mind justice.

At times he wishes he could tell the world about himself and his family, but he and his mother both know humanity isn't ready for that kind of thing, so they stick with their vow and keep it to themselves; as they should.

So, Doctor Susan's senses were right. There was and still is something definitely different about Mark. It just wasn't what she had thought it was, and it's too bad that she had turned out to be the crazy, jealous psycho that she was, because she just might have found out what it really was about him that was so different.

41

Over time, thousands of years, because Mark's DNA had a 0.0001% chemical difference as compared to the DNA of the humans of Earth, when it combined with Andrea's, and their offspring were born, they were different. There were no apparent physical differences or defects, but their intellect and level of intelligence was more evolved. They were smarter, they had a faster level of learning, they were less violent, they were more independent, and they functioned with a higher level of reasoning and awareness. Andrea had always thought that they were just gifted, but Mark knew better. He could never prove it either, nor would he have ever said why, but deep down inside he knew why, and so did his mother. But they swore to never say anything, and they took their secret to their grave. Eventually, throughout generations after generations, because of Mark, Andrea, and their offspring, the humanity of Earth evolved into a new, smarter, faster, higher-level, thinking species. Boundaries fell, war ended, disease was gone, pain, suffering and poverty ceased to exist, and Earth became one. They populated the Solar System and other distant star systems, and met other intelligent species from other worlds. Eventually, the weaker primitive species of humans, the ones that never seemed to get certain aspects of living freely right, without even knowing what had happened to them, peacefully died out. Somebody with a properly functioning brain stopped acting like a self-righteous idiot, and they also finally figured out health care. No one ever knew who it was that figured it out though. But believe it or not? The health care thing did actually happen.

The end…

Author Bio

David Swarbrick is 42 years old. He's a full-time writer and a part-time theoretical physicist. He lives in a small house on the coast of Lake Huron. He has a wife and a son. In his spare time he creates music and studies astronomy…

www.davidswarbrick.webs.com

www.davidswarbrick.webs.com

Author's Books

Happy Root Beer

Every day boys and girls come into the store to buy Happy Root Beer. One day, all the root beer bottles were all bought up. Yet, nobody seems to want to buy Mr. Root Beer. This makes him really sad. Who will come along and help him solve his problem? Join new author David Swarbrick in helping Mr. Root Beer find a new friend to help overcome his loneliness

Peggy's Play House

"Peggy's Play House, a story told by the sun, the moon, the clouds and stars, and even a mouse. It is such a wonderful place to play. Won't you come and read along while we share a warm wonderful day?"

"Oh Yay! We're all going to Peggy's Play House to play!"

Twenty Goofy Gumballs

One day after earning his allowance, Tommy wanted to spend it on gumballs. So his family walked to the corner store and quickly found themselves falling into a silly adventure of collecting and counting. Join author, David E. Swarbrick, Tommy, and his family in an amazing adventure of collecting and counting...

The Journey To Eden

"4,000 years ago an elder chief named Walking Tall, who lived in a different galaxy on a large and far away planet, sat at a sacred fire with his young grandson and told him an amazing story of love and triumph that began a long, long time ago.

Join Walking Tall and his grandson, Stalking Crow, by the sacred fire and listen while the twisting story of a warriors journey to Eden unfolds."

"Captain on the bridge!"

"Commander Report!"

"Aye, Sir, we have two unidentified vessels holding position over our bow."

"So let me guess, you're the biblical devil that I've read about?"

"The diary devise was found on Mars wasn't it?"

"People of Earth, a terrible tragedy has fallen upon us."

"Congratulations Elizabeth, you're having twins."

The Final Breakdown

"Inside this book you will find three short tantalizing stories that are written in the imaginative way that no other author besides David could write them.

Thank you and please enjoy."

www.ingramcontent.com/pod-product-compliance
Lightning Source LLC
Chambersburg PA
CBHW030317080526
44584CB00012B/604